I HAVE INSTALLED *my King*

The King of Israel and
Creation, the Nations and the Last Days

MARTIN SHOUB

I HAVE INSTALLED MY KING: The King of Israel
and Creation, the Nations, and the Last Days

Copyright © 2018 by Martin Shoub

Cover design by Elisha Isabelle Photography & Design
Cover photograph: The Eastern Gate, Jerusalem.
Photography by Martin Shoub

ISBN: 978-1722702342

CONTENTS

ACKNOWLEDGEMENTS

This book project began seven years ago. At that time I was in the midst of my masters' program. I was greatly influenced by my professor, Dr. Mark Kinzer's lectures, particularly on Yeshua's covenant faithfulness to the Jewish people through his ongoing and eternal reign as king of Israel. Around the same time, I heard a wonderful message by Asher Intrater on John 18:37. This verse records Yeshua's answer to Pilate's question regarding his kingly status. Yeshua explained to Pilate, "for this reason I was born." Asher's message steered me into a good deal of contemplation on Yeshua's Kingship.

Dr. Kinzer and Asher Intrater have had a significant impact on my thinking about Yeshua's identity as king. Whatever I have written on the subject that is truthful reflects their influence – if I have been amiss at any point, it is solely my mistake.

I want to thank Dr. Dan Juster for vetting this document for theological errors; his willingness to do so is a great blessing to me. Dr. Kinzer made some helpful criticisms that I have sought to incorporate in the book.

FOREWORD

Marty Shoub has written a book that strongly presents the plan of salvation. "I have Installed My King" agrees with the best of scholarship today, and is also in line with a Messianic Jewish perspective on the Bible. Not only does it trace, as Walter Kaiser calls it, the promised plan of God through the Bible, but it shows the nature of the purpose of Israel, and the progression of history to the first great climax of Israel's history, the coming of the rightful King and the breaking in of the Kingdom of God. The book gives a much stronger vibrant meaning of salvation than simply pardon for sin. Pardon for sin is wonderful but it is not the end goal. Salvation is something great and glorious in the reign of Yeshua. Marty covers the big themes of Messianic Jewish perspectives for the whole Church.

The right teaching derived from the Bible has to begin with the right hermeneutic (the philosophy of interpretation). Our author is very clear that he accepts the Bible in its straightforward contextual meaning. What impresses me about Marty Shoub is that he handles the text so well and accurately! He builds his interpretations step by step on the meaning of the Hebrew Bible in context and always interprets the meaning of the New Testament in keeping with the meaning of the Hebrew text.

The New Testament provides additions to the Hebrew Bible; new and unexpected directions in history, but nothing that changes the meaning of the original texts in the Hebrew Bible. All that is stated there is true, and all its promises to Israel will be fulfilled just as stated. In keeping with this understanding Marty's interpretation of the Bible rings true, the plan of God for Israel and the Church in the last days is clear and founded on the rock solid evidence of what the text says.

"I Have Installed My King" presents an outline of that Kingdom salvation, and the meaning of this era of Jew and

Gentile being in communion together in Yeshua. This leads to the next great climax, the return of the King to earth to rule and reign from Jerusalem. The events leading up to this are also noted. The book presents us with a grand sweep. It is such a good read, but not difficult in language or concept. It is easy to grasp. I am glad to recommend this book.

Daniel Juster, Th. D. Restoration from Zion of Tikkun Int., Visiting Professor, The King's University.

INTRODUCTION

The beginning of Yeshua's preaching ministry commences with the words, *"The time is fulfilled, and the kingdom of God is at hand; repent and believe in the gospel"* (Mark. 1:15). Yeshua spoke about the kingdom of God more than any other topic. *"Your kingdom come "*(Matt. 6:10), is the first petition of the model prayer Yeshua taught his disciples. Yeshua's emphasis on the kingdom of God alerts us to its significance and the high priority it occupied in Yeshua's teaching ministry. Usually he taught about the kingdom through parables. Parables present word pictures that allow for hues and shades of meaning beyond what direct, straightforward teaching can provide.

Very often Yeshua would describe the kingdom of God by comparing it to an object or by telling a brief story. To say, *"The kingdom of heaven is like a grain of mustard seed..."* (Matt. 13:31), does not explain everything there is to know about the kingdom, but it activates the creative side of our brains and allows for a richness of meaning far beyond saying "the kingdom starts out small but eventually grows to be very big."

Whenever we are describing matters related to God and eternity we are in a sense speaking of things beyond our full comprehension. One cannot describe the kingdom of God as if it were boundaries on a map or a human institution. Whenever we talk about the Kingdom of God we are considering a mystery.

Mysteries are more so revealed then explained. That is why parables also serve as a means to divide those to whom the mystery has been revealed from those who have not been given the revelation. Yeshua said, *"To you it has been given to know the secret [Gk. musterion] of the kingdom of heaven, but to them it has not been given"* (Matt. 13:11). Yeshua explained why he spoke in parables by quoting from Isaiah 6:9,10: *"Keep on hearing, but do not understand; keep on seeing, but do not perceive.' Make the heart of this people dull, and their ears heavy, and blind their eyes; lest they see with their eyes, and hear with their ears, and understand with their hearts, and turn and be healed."*

The failure of the Jewish people to see, hear and understand has had tremendous significance with respect to the role of the Jewish people in salvation history.[1] However, for our purposes it is enough to recognize that the kingdom of God has a mysterious dimension.

Perhaps you have read books or heard sermons entitled something like, "the mystery of the kingdom" or "the secret of the kingdom." Typically, these messages are centered on concepts and principles. Very often in church circles the kingdom of God is described with reference to concepts, i.e. the culture of the kingdom, the principles of the kingdom, the dynamics of the kingdom, etc. We have all seen or heard these sorts of titles regarding the kingdom of God.

This is not to say there are no conceptual components to God's kingdom, but I fear many of us have missed the central aspect of what is the kingdom. There is some mystery to it to be sure, but the basic meaning is very simple. The kingdom of God is the rule of God. It is the realm under God's ruling authority. To pray, *"Thy kingdom come"* is to pray *"Thy will be done on earth as it is in heaven."* The earth has always been the intended realm of God's rule. This is true because God created the earth:

> *"The earth is the LORD's and the fullness thereof, the world and those who dwell therein, for he has founded it upon the seas and established it upon the rivers."* (Ps. 24:1–2)

As the Creator, God owns the earth and everything (and everyone) that dwells therein. God chose Israel as His special treasure over all peoples because, as He put it, *"all the earth is mine"* (Exod. 19:5). As the Creator He has the authority to

---

[1] See, Martin Shoub, "To The Jew First: The Formation of One New Man" (San Bernardino, CA: CreateSpace. 2017) In this book I address Israel's failure to receive Messiah and its ramifications for the salvation of the nations.

choose. He chose Israel for His purposes; He sets up and takes down rulers for the same reasons (Dan. 4:17).

Creators decide what to do with their creation. Paintings don't object to the artist's choice of colour, musical instruments don't determine which notes to sound and pots don't complain to potters, *"Why have you made me like this?"* (Isa. 45:9; Rom. 9:20). The creation mandate that bestowed authority to rule onto humanity never removed God's ultimate authority over creation. The command to have dominion over the planet and its creatures (Gen. 1:26), did not release mankind to have ultimate control and authority over the earth. The authority to rule was a delegated authority under God's over-arching rule.

This command to rule, or "have dominion" can be understood as a covenant relationship between Adam, Eve and the Almighty. The first couple were the Creator's regents ruling on His behalf. They were God's representatives on earth.

Later in history, after Adam's rule was marred by sin the delegated authority to represent God on earth was bestowed upon Israel's descendants. This expectation to obey the Creator and follow His mandate was centred in one distinct people group. Israel was to display the Creator's dominion over creation by following His commandments and thus rising above all peoples in blessings, prosperity and power. Israel was intended to be a showcase to all the nations, demonstrating the truth and propriety of the Creator's commands and judgements. God's expectation of Israel to reveal His authority on earth through obedience was further refined and delegated to the king of Israel. Israel's king was to rule over the nation through obedience to God's commandments. The king was to copy out his own scroll of the Torah, and to read it *"all the days of his life"* (Deut. 17:19). In the same way that God ratified these expectations of obedience by covenant with the nation, so also this expectation for Israel's king to rule on God's behalf was ratified by covenant between God and David.

The king of Israel was to obey God and follow God's commands. The covenant promise made to David was that one of David's descendants would rule over the house of Israel forever.

11

This enduring rule over Israel was later expanded to include rulership over all nations. The kingdom of God on earth was under the authority of God's appointed ruler, namely the son of David whose rule would never end.

Israel's prophets presented a vision of the kingdom of God as the rule of God over the whole planet, under the administration of Israel's king, God's Messiah. The kingdom they described was not a spiritual, inner reign over individuals submitted to the rule of God. The prophetic scriptures describe the kingdom as tangible and concrete. It occurs on earth and effects all of creation. The eternal king of Israel, the Messiah rules over the planet from Jerusalem.

Yeshua did not abrogate this vision of God's rule over the planet but he expanded it to include an inward dimension. The rule of God was also intended for the human heart. The New Covenant, enacted through Yeshua's death and resurrection writes the holy Torah of God on the human heart. This is an inward transformation activated by the Holy Spirit's ministry within us. The Holy Spirit motivates us from the inside out to submit to God's rule. This internal dimension of the kingdom was established through Yeshua's priestly ministry.

Yeshua himself proclaimed, *"All authority in heaven and earth has been give to me"* (Matt. 28:18), nothing has been left outside of his control. But at present, we do not see everything under Yeshua's control; all powers in heaven and earth are not yet submitted to his reign. As the writer of Hebrews observed:

> *"Now in putting everything in subjection to him, he left nothing outside his control. At present, we do not yet see everything in subjection to him. But we see him who for a little while was made lower than the angels, namely Jesus, crowned with glory and honour because of the suffering of death, so that by the grace of God he might taste death for everyone."* (Heb. 2:8–9)

As Yeshua explained to the disciples on the road to Emmaus, the Messiah had to suffer in order to enter his glory (Luke 24:26).

God's Messiah, His appointed king is also a priest, a saviour who interceded on our behalf, not just with prayers, and not as priests before him by offerings of animals and grains but with his own blood and broken body. This saving act - the king Messiah taking the lowest place by submitting to death on a cross is the central act that validates Yeshua as God's ruler. Because he gave up everything including his life, all things come under his control and authority. We can only marvel and worship.

This is a matter so deep with meaning we can never fully plumb the depths of its significance. As followers of Yeshua we follow him in death in the waters of baptism, and we remember his death as he commanded us, when we participate in his body and blood through the bread and wine of communion. Yeshua's saving sacrificial death can never be understated. Commanded by an angel in a dream, Joseph (Yoseph) named Mary's (Miriam's) son Yeshua, because he would save his people from their sins (Matt. 1:21).[2] His name for all eternity bears witness to this saving act and his priestly ministry.

Yeshua's glory as saviour does not overshadow his glory as king. It would be foolish to pit Yeshua's role as saviour against his role as king. He is both. However, within the vast majority of Christian proclamation it would seem that far more attention is focused on Yeshua as saviour than Yeshua as king. I would contend that the message of the Scriptures places greater emphasis on Yeshua as king. Even in communion, where we contemplate the awesome sacrifice of Yeshua's death, we do so *until he comes"* (1 Cor. 11:26), and he will come again as king.

Yeshua bears the marks of his crucifixion for eternity. But for eternity he sits enthroned as king with all authority. His priesthood is the wondrous ministry that opens the way for us to join him in his rule. In God's appointed order, Yeshua's priesthood is necessary to fulfill his mandate as ruler. Because he offered himself in priestly service, Yeshua restored his Heavenly Father's creation mandate for all humanity to rule over the planet.

---

[2] The name Yeshua, Heb. (ישוע) is derived from the Hebrew word for salvation, Yeshuah, Heb. (ישועה)

Yeshua is God's appointed ruler but wonder of wonders, he will share his rule with us. In order to make this so, Yeshua serves in the "heavenly Temple" as God's eternal priest. His intercessory atonement works salvation for us, those appointed to be his joint heirs.

Yeshua's priesthood does not end with his ascension into heaven. As the scriptures declare, Yeshua "is a priest forever." (Ps. 110:4). In the temple service, the priests not only offered sacrifices for sin but burnt offerings and peace offerings as well. Priestly sacrifices were not only necessary to provide atonement for sin; they served as a means of worship and fellowship with the God of Israel. Yeshua's priestly ministry continues in heaven as the High Priest after the order of Melchizedek who assures "our peaceful fellowship with the Most High for all eternity."[3]

Yeshua is not just king in the generic sense. He is a king according to lineage over a specific people, in a specific land. His rule over the planet extends out of his covenant identity as the king of Israel. It is the king of Israel who is promised dominion over all nations. Therefore, Yeshua is king of kings because he is king of Israel. He is not king of Israel because he is king of kings.

This book is primarily about Yeshua as God's appointed king. As the angel Gabriel proclaimed, *"He will reign over the House of Jacob forever"* (Luke 1:33). Yeshua is Israel's eternal ruler but Yeshua's rule extends beyond Israel. As Daniel saw in his vision of heavens throne room, *"And to him was given dominion and glory and a kingdom, that all peoples, nations, and languages should serve him"* (Dan. 7:14).

This book will explore how the kingdom of God and the kingdom of Israel fit within the Creator's original mandate to bestow the rulership of planet earth to humankind, that special creature that He created in His own image and likeness. It is a true story filled with majesty and hope beyond any other. It is indeed the good news of the kingdom.

---

[3] My thanks to Dr. Mark Kinzer
for this helpful comment from an email received July 1, 2018.

Part 1

The King of Israel and Creation

CHAPTER 1

The Creation Mandate

The apex of the creation account is when God proclaims His intention to make a creature (man) in His image and likeness (Gen. 1:26). The text does not include a description or definition of what constitutes God's image in the creature. What follows is a functional expectation for the godlike creature, man.[4]

> *"And let them have dominion over the fish of the sea and over the birds of the heavens and over the livestock and over all the earth and over every creeping thing that creeps on the earth."* (Gen. 1:26)

Functionally, to be made in God's image is to rule. One could say that God created a creature in His image and likeness for the purpose of ruling over all that He had previously made. Put simply, men and women were created to rule. This in no way exhausts the depth of meaning contained in being created in God's image. By extension and implication, we can draw a tremendous amount of description and insight into the profound meaning of being created in God's image. Whatever else constitutes God's image in humanity, according to the text, the direct application of bearing this image is the capacity to rule.

The creation account in Genesis 1 is marked by sublime tranquility and orderliness. *"The earth was without form and void."* (Gen. 1:2) The Hebrew conveys the sense of emptiness and

---

[4] The only description in Genesis 1 for God's image in man is that the creature made in God's image is constituted as both male and female (Gen. 1:27).

17

waste, confusion and disorder.[5] God speaks and that which was without form takes on shape, the cosmos that was chaotic emptiness takes on order. In contrast, competing pagan cosmologies describe creation as the unintended outcome of the battle between primordial gods. There is no suggestion of purpose or absolute sovereignty. The beings that become the pantheon of gods defeat the primordial monsters and the earth sprang out of the corpse of the vanquished foe.[6] In the biblical account, from beginning to end God Himself is the only actor. All proceeds according to His direction and only He evaluates the outcome.

The natural world does not require a special creature to manage and rule over it. Ecosystems untouched by human intervention function without difficulty. There are contemporary voices that regard human beings as the flaw in the system. One does not have to look very hard to see how humans have injured the natural order of things through our carelessness and lack of foresight. Yet it was the Creator's intention for humans to rule over the very good creation He had made. Specifically, the man was placed in the garden *"to work it and keep it"* (Gen. 2:15). The command to rule recorded in Genesis 1:28 includes the command to multiply and fill the earth. By extension, the working and keeping responsibility would then apply to every physical location where humanity would eventually spread.

As Creator, God has ultimate authority over creation. Just as the potter has authority over the clay and a composer over the musical score, the Creator has absolute freedom over the creation.

---

[5] Isaiah 34:11 includes the same two Hebrew words translated in Genesis 1:2 as "without form and void" — tohu, vohu (תהו, בהו). The ESV translates tohu and vohu in Isaiah 34:11 respectively as confusion and emptiness.

[6] In the Babylonian creation account, The Enuma Elish, the chief god Marduk, having overcome the primordial monster Tiamat, cuts her body in two, creating the heavens and the earth from her divided halves. J.V. Kinnier Wilson. "The Epic of Creation." In Documents from Old Testament Times, D. Winton Thomas, Editor. New York: Harper, 1961. 10,11

The Book of Job addresses the authority of God as Creator. Throughout Job's ordeal he complained that he should have been able to question God regarding his terrible misfortunes: *"But I would speak to the Almighty, and I desire to argue my case with God"* (Job 13:3).[7]

When God finally condescended to meet with Job He never answered any of Job's questions; the Creator is not under any obligation to provide answers to His creatures. Instead, The Almighty turned the tables on Job, demanding Job answer the questions:

> *"Dress for action like a man; I will question you, and you make it known to me. 'Where were you when I laid the foundation of the earth? Tell me, if you have understanding. Who determined its measurements - surely you know!'"* (Job 38:3-5)

What follows is example after example of God's sovereignty as Creator. God has every right to do with Job as He sees fit. He is under no obligation to explain His actions to Job or anyone else because He is the Creator and Job is the creature.

When the Apostles were facing threats to their mission, when earthly authorities commanded them to cease proclaiming the gospel they appealed to God's sovereignty as Creator.

> *"When they were released, they went to their friends and reported what the chief priests and the elders had said to them. And when they heard it, they lifted their voices together to God and said, 'Sovereign Lord, who made the heaven and the earth and the sea and everything in them...Lord, look upon their threats and grant to your servants to continue to speak your word with all boldness, while you stretch out your hand to heal, and signs and wonders are performed through the name of your holy servant Jesus.'"* (Acts 4:23–30)

---

[7] For other examples see Job 16:21; 19:6,7; 23:3-5; 31:35

God has given authority for mankind to rule over creation but this never abrogates God's ultimate authority over creation as the Creator. Mankind's authority to rule is a delegated authority. Humanity's dominion over creation is not absolute; our government over the planet is accountable to heaven's rule.

Delegation is God's pattern of authority. The story of Yeshua and the centurion illustrates heaven's authority grid. Responding to the centurion's appeal on behalf of his servant ill at home, Yeshua determined to travel to the centurion's house to heal his servant.

The centurion politely objected on the grounds that he was not worthy to welcome Yeshua under his roof. He then said something so profound that Matthew recorded, Yeshua *"marvelled"* at this response (Matt. 8:10). The centurion acknowledged all Yeshua needed to do was speak a word and his servant would be healed. The centurion was certain this was so because as a Roman officer he knew something about authority.

Most of us are familiar with the story of Yeshua and the centurion. Before continuing I think it is instructive to first consider what Yeshua had to say about the Roman authority structure: *"But Jesus called them to him and said, 'You know that the rulers of the Gentiles lord it over them, and their great ones exercise authority over them'"* (Matt. 20:25).

The primary characteristic of the Roman authority structure is the ruler exercising authority over his subjects. The one in charge decides and is not accountable to others. Caesar did what Caesar chose to do - the same was true for Pharaoh and all Ancient Near East despots. Modern authority structures have accountabilities built into the system, but still our contemporary worldview places a high value on autonomy and the freedom to choose according to one's own conscience and values. We all aspire to sing, "I did it my way."

The centurion had a unique perspective. One would expect a Roman officer to explain that there was no need for Yeshua to personally attend to his servant at his villa because, like Yeshua he was a man "of authority." Rather, he remarked that he was a man "under authority." He explained that because he was under authority he would tell one, *"Go,' and he goes, and to another, 'Come,' and he comes, and to [his] servant, 'Do this,' and he does it"* (Matt. 8:9).

The centurion understood a truth about authority that made Yeshua marvel. True authority is not to be over others but to be under the only one who has complete authority. True authority is delegated authority. The centurion also recognized something about Yeshua that marked him as a man of great faith. He recognized that Yeshua was also a man under authority, the authority Yeshua had to heal someone was not his own. Yeshua was demonstrating the power of the kingdom as one "under authority."

This is Yeshua's testimony of himself:

> *"Truly, truly, I say to you, the Son can do nothing of his own accord, but only what he sees the Father doing. For whatever the Father does, that the Son does likewise."* (John 5:19)

> *"I can do nothing on my own. As I hear, I judge, and my judgment is just, because I seek not my own will but the will of him who sent me."* (John 5:30)

> *"For I have come down from heaven, not to do my own will but the will of him who sent me."* (John 6:38)

In always doing the will of his Heavenly Father, Yeshua not only reflects his eternal function as the divine Son who does the will of the Father, but also as the representative head of humanity, and the representative head of Israel. Both Adam and the king of Israel were required to obey the Father, and in a sense were both the "Son" of God.[8] Yeshua is the "Last Adam" because he is the head of a new humanity, and also because he functioned according to God's expectations for the first Adam.

---

[8] See, Luke 3:38; 2 Sam. 7:14

21

The First Adam[9] was given authority to rule. But like the authority exercised by Yeshua, this authority was delegated. Like Yeshua, Adam was also to only do the will of Him who sent him. The bestowal of authority on Adam came with the expectation to multiply and populate the earth and to subdue it. The sense here is all that is under Adam's authority is to be made subject to his will.[10] Curiously, there is only one negative commandment. Adam was not to eat of the tree of the knowledge of good and evil (Gen. 2:17).

To rule over a kingdom as vast and complex as all of planet earth would require a great deal of wisdom and knowledge. Adam was given the authority to rule but not the tools to make decisions. The most elemental function of governance is to do good and curtail evil. Solomon's prayer for wisdom exemplified this basic requirement:

> *"O LORD my God, you have made your servant king in place of David my father, although I am but a little child. I do not know how to go out or come in. And your servant is in the midst of your people whom you have chosen, a great people, too many to be numbered or counted for multitude. Give your servant therefore an understanding mind to govern your people, that I may discern between good and evil, for who is able to govern this your great people?"* (1 Kings 3:7–9)

Solomon understood that the task of governing the nation of Israel was too much for him. He asked for the wisdom to discern between good and evil, to apply the knowledge of good and evil

---

[9] I refer to Adam the man because he is the counter to Yeshua, the last Adam. However, the authority to rule was given both to Adam and Eve. Both the man and the woman were responsible for the choices they made. All my comments about Adam apply to Eve as well.

[10] The Hebrew verb, *kabash* (כבש) implies forcing the object into submission. See, entry 951,951a. Theological Wordbook of the Old Testament (TWOT), R. Laird Harris, Editor; Gleason L. Archer, Jr., Associate Editor; Bruce K. Waltke, Associate Editor Copyright © 1980 by The Moody Bible Institute of Chicago Electronic text used by permission.

with a wisdom imparted from heaven. This request pleased the LORD, and showed Solomon to be a man of noble character and humility. If Solomon needed supernatural discernment to rule over Israel, how much more so would Adam and Eve have required discernment to rule over the whole planet? And yet though in plain sight for Adam to apprehend, the provision for discernment was prohibited to him. How would Adam rule over the planet, and how could he subdue it without the knowledge of good and evil?

Solomon was an example of how even divinely imparted wisdom cannot ensure wise rule. Solomon knew good and evil far better than any human before him. He tested the limits of both wisdom and folly (Eccl. 2:12); he explored the depths of good and evil without restraint and concluded, *"all is vanity and striving after wind"* (Eccl. 1:14). Like the first Adam, his access to the fruit of the tree of the knowledge of good and evil did not result in wise rule. Despite having the knowledge of what was good and what was evil, Solomon ultimately failed because he chose to be the final arbitrator of how to apply that knowledge. The serpent's promise that partaking of the fruit would make the humans to *"be like God"* (Gen. 3:5) was a cruel deception.

The truth was, Adam and Eve were already "like" God. They were made in God's image and likeness. What the Serpent was really offering them was the ability to become independent of God, deciding good and evil for themselves without relying on God's good and perfect will to guide them.

However, knowing good and evil does not assure one will choose the good and shun the evil. The only assurance of doing good is to submit to God's rule. Only the Creator has the wisdom, power, goodness and foresight to know the consequences for every action, and the character to always choose what is best. Adam did not require the knowledge of good and evil to rule because his rule was to be in complete submission to his Heavenly Father. What the Father determined was the good path was the way Adam was to proceed. He was to only do what he saw his Heavenly Father doing. He was never to be the final arbitrator of good and evil. Adam's submission to his all wise, all good

23

Heavenly Father would have assured that his rule would have been just, wise and good.

The path set for Adam and Eve they failed to tread. They did not rule in submission to their Heavenly Father. They did not rule through the good imparted to them from God. Instead, they chose to decide for themselves what was good and what was evil. This choosing had a tremendous impact on how they understood themselves, the world around them and the God who made them both. There was no turning back from this decision, and we all have been living with the consequences ever since.

In contrast, the Last Adam administered authority according to the pattern originally set for the first Adam. Yeshua did what Adam failed to do. Yeshua did what he saw his Father doing, spoke what he heard his Father say, and judged according to his Father's direction.

Adam's rule was to be marked by a love relationship between Adam and his Heavenly Father. This relationship would have resulted in perfect obedience and a complete lack of wilfulness. Originally, Adam did not need to be able to discern between good and evil because he was to rely exclusively on God's wisdom. His rule would always choose the good because he would always choose God's way. He would not need to experience good and evil in order to know what to choose and what to avoid because in obedience to the good God, Adam would always choose the good way.

The human condition, such as it is post fall, functions in most cases through individuals and societies learning what is good by experiencing the consequences of good choices and bad choices. We learn by the knowledge of good and evil.

The temptation laid out by the serpent was that God's intended rulership arrangement was somehow a withholding. If Eve did not eat then somehow she was blind. Her capacity to choose for herself would be severely constrained. Partaking of the tree of the knowledge of good and evil would open her eyes to give her godlike power to discern for herself what is good and what is evil. The narration explains that the tree *"was to be desired to make one wise."* (Gen. 3:6)

In a sense, partaking of the fruit was a removal of restriction. After both Eve and Adam had eaten, *"the eyes of both were opened, and they knew they were naked"* (Gen. 3:7). They had become more like God in the sense that now they had the capacity to be the final arbitrators of good and evil. They no longer required God's wisdom to choose the good, they could decide for themselves. However, this most unfortunate predicament of eating the fruit of the tree of the knowledge of good and evil did not make them godlike in the way they perhaps had hoped it would. They lacked the wisdom and the all-encompassing love that pervades the Godhead. Their ability to choose did not endow them with the capacity to choose the good way. They would have to learn through experience.

Their capacity to choose the good was further hampered by the most disastrous consequences of their disobedience. As they had individually become the final arbitrators of good and evil they lost the relational connection to creation, to each other and to God. They had become autonomous. Even the Godhead is not autonomous in the sense that the One God exists in three persons. There is mutuality, there is oneness, and there is love. An autonomous being does not know oneness because he/she does not know mutuality. Therefore, the first realization after partaking of the fruit of the tree was that they were naked.

Previously, the narrative explained they were naked and unashamed (Gen. 2:25). Now, they knew they were apart from one another. This realization of being naked before the other, this sense of being separate and autonomous beings moved them to cover themselves. They no longer experienced oneness. The consequences of this have brought untold suffering upon humanity. As individual final arbitrators of good and evil we no longer enjoy true oneness. The grid of consideration narrows down to what is good or what is evil for me. My good may be evil for you and your good may be evil for me. But as individual final arbitrators of good and evil we do not consider good with respect to mutuality and oneness.

This separating off extrapolates beyond individual considerations to family groups, ethnicities, nations, and genders.

25

We identify ourselves apart from others, apart from creation and most tragically, apart from God. We are no longer comfortable being naked before God and before others because now we have an individualized self-interest, and an individualized sense of our own determination of what is good and what is evil.

CHAPTER 2

The Mandate Lost

The temptation to choose for oneself what is good and what is evil, to become the final determiner of will, is a temptation promising an expectation of freedom. The serpent goaded Eve by accusing God of knowingly withholding godlike capacity from her, *"For God knows that when you eat of it your eyes will be opened, and you will be like God, knowing good and evil"* (Gen. 3:5). In a very narrow sense, the prohibition against eating of the Tree of the knowledge of good and evil was a restriction. God's own internal dialogue agrees with the serpent's assessment:

> *"Then the LORD God said, "Behold, the man has become like one of us in knowing good and evil. Now, lest he reach out his hand and take also of the tree of life and eat, and live forever—"therefore the LORD God sent him out from the garden of Eden to work the ground from which he was taken"* (Gen. 3:22–23)

However, in this scenario *"to be like God,"* knowing good and evil was not a benefit to Adam and Eve. Their newly gained capacity to choose far outstripped their inherent abilities to manage this newfound knowledge. True freedom is not the ability to choose. True freedom is following the good path. True freedom is only found through obedience to God. The freedom to choose has inherent consequences. The universe is ordered by the wisdom and goodness of God. Any choice that deviates from this godly order is by definition out of order. One could say that such a choice misses the mark of God's order.[11]

Failure to choose the godly way, or the good, is sin. Choosing sin not only results in the negative consequences that follow missing God's order, but also a bondage upon the will of the one who chooses the bad path. Scripture testifies that through Adam's example of disobedience, all creation was subjected to bondage (Rom. 5:18,19; 8:19-21). Both Yeshua and later Paul explained that the act of sinning compels one to sin the more.

> *"Truly, truly, I say to you, everyone who practices sin is a slave to sin."* (John 8:34)

> *"Do you not know that if you present yourselves to anyone as obedient slaves, you are slaves of the one whom you obey, either of sin, which leads to death, or of obedience, which leads to righteousness?"* (Romans 6:16)

Freedom to choose is only truly a benefit when one chooses what is good. The final arbitrator of what is good is not human wisdom, conscience or desire but the word of God. God promised Israel a blessed life on the basis of Israel's obedience. If Israel chose the good way they were blessed. Conversely, if they chose a way apart from the will of God they suffered negative consequences.

Israel's blessings and curses were tied into Israel's national covenant status as the nation chosen to represent God to all nations. But the principle of blessing for obedience to the revealed will of God, and consequences for failing to abide within the constraints of the good way still held sway over all human endeavour. The blessings and curses associated with obedience and disobedience to the will of God reaches back to the beginning of human history. This is not just a reward/punishment scenario.

---

[11] The Hebrew word for sin, chata (חטא) can convey the idea of missing the target or destination. See, Judg. 20:16; Prov. 19:2

The way of sin brings it own negative consequences because sin is out of alignment with the divine order.

Regrettably, with the choice to partake of the fruit of the tree of the knowledge of good and evil, the pull towards disobedience entered into the human condition. The Genesis account of the fall describes this as an alienation that separated human beings from one another, from the environment and from the Creator. Adam and Eve recognized they were naked and consequently, they were ashamed. Their oneness had been shattered. They originally had not been ashamed because they enjoyed a sense of oneness and connection. Neither saw themselves as completely distinct and apart from each other.

Their original connectedness was not an absence of individual identity, but the oneness that they experienced as made in the image of the one God. The oneness Yeshua prayed for on behalf of His disciples, *"that they may all be one, just as you, Father, are in me, and I in you,"* (John 17:21), was the original reality for humanity. Adam was in Eve as Eve was in Adam. However, this all changed with the fall. The narrative now describes a distinctiveness that betrayed a newfound alienation from one another.

When God called Adam to account, asking if he had eaten from the prohibited tree Adam shifted responsibility on to Eve:

> *"The man said, 'The woman whom you gave to be with me, she gave me fruit of the tree, and I ate.'"* (Gen. 3:12)

Likewise, when Eve was called to account she shifted the blame to the serpent:

> *"The woman said, 'The serpent deceived me, and I ate.'"* (Gen. 3:13)

Their individualized sense of self, and their instinctive reaction to deflect blame onto another betrayed a shift in their consciousness. The couple that was *"naked and unashamed"* would have no concept of seeing themselves uniquely apart and separate from the other. It would have been unthinkable for them to deflect blame, as if consequences for the one could be escaped by an expectation of consequences solely on the other. Originally they had no sense of a consequence for the one apart from its same consequence for the other.

After the fall, each individual became the determiner of what was good. In this scenario, what is good for one may not be good for the other. Without divine revelation of the good path, the path aligned with God's order, the ability to choose the right way is hindered by each one's inherent disconnect from others. If I am the final arbitrator of good and evil, I can only decide based on my own interests. What is good for me may not be good for you. This extends to every level of relationship including people groups and nation states.

The biblical narrative illustrates this condition through Cain's response to the Creator's inquiry as to the whereabouts of his brother Abel. Cain answers the Almighty, *"I do not know; am I my brother's keeper?"* (Gen. 4:9). From Cain's perspective, his interests as an individual did not extend to any obligation to his brother. The oneness existing within the Godhead that was to be reflected in the creature made in the divine image, was so severely truncated, Cain could dismiss Almighty God with an assumption that it was not his business to know the whereabouts of his brother. Cain was for Cain and not for Abel or anyone else.

Despite Cain's grievous violation of the Creator's order, God still showed him mercy. Cain was punished by exile but his life was spared. To ensure that no others took vengeance on him, God decreed sevenfold retribution upon anyone who would exact revenge on Cain (Gen. 4:15). Divine justice was served according to divine wisdom, mercy and goodness.

Four generations later, Lamech, Cains's great grandson also committed murder. Lamech did not seek God's mercy. Instead, Lamech issued his own decree, determining that his own measure of justice should exceed that of the Creator.

30

"Lamech said to his wives: "Adah and Zillah, hear my voice; you wives of Lamech, listen to what I say: I have killed a man for wounding me, a young man for striking me. If Cain's revenge is sevenfold, then Lamech's is seventy-sevenfold." (Gen. 4:23–24)

Lamech determined that if God had decreed sevenfold retribution on anyone who tried to take vengeance against Cain for murdering his brother, then Lamech is worthy of seventy-seven fold retribution for the same offence. Lamech became the arbitrator of justice according to his own will, quite apart from submission to the Creator's justice, or even an appeal to the Creator's mercy. Lamech was exercising dominion in the earth, but not according to the divine plan. His dominion was determined by his own sense of what was good and what was evil. Lamech became a law unto himself.

However, Lamech's independent rule was not really independent. As stated above, yielding to sin puts one in bondage to sin. Adam was given dominion to rule over the planet. This dominion was not an independent rule, but a rule as regent in submission to the Creator. When Adam chose to be independent of God's rule he did not achieve his desired end. Instead of submission to the only wise God, *"merciful and gracious, slow to anger, and abounding in steadfast love and faithfulness"* (Exod. 34:6), he subjected himself to another master, a master of lies and cruelty whose only interest is *"to steal and kill and destroy"* (John 10:10).

Yeshua's temptation in the wilderness provides a clue to this master/servant relationship between mankind and Satan began with Adam's disobedience:

"And the devil took him up and showed him all the kingdoms of the world in a moment of time, and said to him, 'To you I will give all this authority and their glory, for it has been delivered to me, and I give it to whom I will. If you, then, will worship me, it will all be yours.'" (Luke 4:5–7)

31

The *"kingdoms of the world"* had not originally been *"delivered"* to the devil. By believing the serpent's lie, the authority originally given to the first couple was in a sense transferred to the serpent, because by yielding to the serpent, the man came under the sway of the serpent's domination.

Paul said it this way:

> *"And you were dead in the trespasses and sins in which you once walked, following the course of this world, following the prince of the power of the air, the spirit that is now at work in the sons of disobedience."* (Eph. 2:1–2)

The choice to rule over the planet in submission to the Creator's will had shifted into a bondage that granted authority over the *"kingdoms of this world"* to the devil. The consequences of the fall go beyond matters of personal freedom and individual corruption. They have far reaching geo-political consequences. The redemption promised as a judgment against the serpent is not only about freeing individuals from their own sinful proclivities, but a restoration of the rule of God over the nations.

As the Creator, God has always ultimately ruled over the nations. But in a real sense, only with the establishment of Messiah's rule over the nations does Satan's rule end: *"Now the salvation and the power and the kingdom of our God and the authority of his Christ have come, for the accuser of our brothers has been thrown down"* (Rev.12:10).

CHAPTER 3

The Promise of Restoration

"The LORD God said to the serpent, 'Because you have done this, cursed are you above all livestock and above all beasts of the field; on your belly you shall go, and dust you shall eat all the days of your life. I will put enmity between you and the woman, and between your offspring and her offspring; he shall bruise your head, and you shall bruise his heel.'" (Gen. 3:14–15)

The fall described in Genesis 3 is a watershed event in the Scriptures. It represents a major divide between humanity's condition in the garden before their disobedience to God's command and life outside the garden afterwards. All that came before can be understood to tell the story of the creation in its ideal state, leading up to the event that caused mankind to be banished from that idyllic Garden of Eden. After the fall, God made curse pronouncements on the man, the woman and the serpent. The curse on the serpent was unique within the curse pronouncements of Genesis 3, because unlike the curse upon the man and the woman, the curse upon the serpent included a promise of restoration - for the man and the woman.

The image of a future seed of the woman that would bruise or crush the Serpent' head, [12] not only anticipated an ongoing antipathy between the serpent and the woman's seed but a final,

---

[12] The Hebrew verb, *shûp* (שׁוּף) is extraordinarily problematic, because it occurs only here and in two other difficult poetic passages: Ps. 139:11, Job 9:17." Depending on context it can mean batter, crush, bruise. Gordon J. Wenham, Genesis 1–15, WBC 1; Accordance electronic ed. (Grand Rapids, MI: Zondervan, 1987), 80. Paul applied the sense of "to crush" in his benediction to the Romans. (Rom. 16:20)

decisive victory over the serpent through the seed of the woman. The term "head" can be understood as a synecdoche for authority and rule. Likewise the pronouncement, *"on your belly you shall go, and dust you shall eat all the days of your life"* (Gen. 3:14), can be understood metaphorically as a promise of ultimate failure and humiliation, rather than a structural change in "the serpent's" anatomy. The same imagery is used to describe Messiah's enemies during his rule over Israel and the nations:

> *"May he have dominion from sea to sea, and from the River*
> *to the ends of the earth! May desert tribes bow down*
> *before him, and his enemies lick the dust!"* (Ps. 72:8–9)

Embedded within the curse on the serpent is the prophetic promise of his ultimate downfall. The *"kingdoms of the world"* that had been *"delivered"* unto him through the fall will ultimately return to a human authority though the seed of the woman. Humanity caused the disruption in divine order for planet earth and a representative of humanity would restore divine order once again. But in the same way that authority over the planet was bestowed on humanity through an act of divine grace, so the restoration through the seed of the woman is also an act of divine grace.

Genesis 3 anticipates the seed of the woman, God's agent of restoration and His champion, to destroy the serpent's usurped authority. As noted above, Genesis 3 is a watershed event within the Scriptures. This is especially so for Christians as we all understand the promised seed of the woman to be Yeshua the Messiah.

In his book, "The God of Israel and Christian Theology" R. Kendall Soulen employed the term, "canonical narrative" to describe the over-arching back-story that melds the Old Testament to the New Testament.[13] Soulen explained that New Testament believers read the Old Testament through the lens of

---

[13] R. Kendall Soulen. "The God of Israel and Christian Theology" (Minneapolis, Minn: Fortress Press, 1996) 25

this canonical narrative, so as to fit the story of the Old Testament within the interpretive framework of the New Testament.

This is not disingenuous, or reading into the text, all of us regardless of our background read the Scriptures with a narrative back-story that shapes our understanding of the text. Rabbinic Judaism also employs a canonical narrative that fits the Hebrew Scriptures within the interpretive framework of the Talmud.[14]

Genesis 3 is a pivotal text within the traditional Christian canonical narrative. Soulen divides the narrative into four "crucial episodes." 1. God created humanity to exercise authority over the earth and its creatures with an intended consummation of humanity to eternal life.[15] 2. Humanity rebels against the Creator. 3. The redemption of humanity through the death and resurrection of the Messiah (anticipated in Genesis 3:15). 4. The final consummation of creation.[16] Within this basic framework Genesis 3 not only describes the fall but also anticipates the redemption. The promise of the seed of the woman who is to come is the programmatic text for everything that follows, all that comes after Genesis 3 is the story of the consequences of the fall and the outworking of the redemption.

Within this narrative, the Hebrew Scriptures following Genesis 3:15 function as the story of how God enacted this promised redemption. The Hebrew Scriptures after Genesis 3:15

---

[14] Jewish Theologian David Novak acknowledged that the Hebrew Scriptures function within rabbinic Judaism vis a vis the Talmud, parallel to the way the "Old Testament" functions for Christians vis a vis the New Testament.
See, David Novak, "From Supersessionism to Parallelism in Jewish-Christian Dialogue" in Jews and Christians: People of God, editors, Carl E. Braaten and Robert W. Jensen (Grand Rapids, MI: Eerdmans, 2003) 109,110.

[15] Soulen, "The God of Israel and Christian Theology" 26.

[16] Soulen, "The God of Israel and Christian Theology" 25. Though the humans were without sin they had not yet to completed God's purposes for creation. They had not extended God's rule across the globe, they had not judged the rebellious angelic powers (Ps. 8:5,6; 1 Cor. 6:3), nor had they partaken of the Tree of Life.

could be understood as a transitory story to bring the reader to Matthew 1:1. In this capacity, Israel serves as a ferry boat to move the story of redemption from the promise of a redeemer made in Genesis 3:15, to the announcement of the Messiah in Matthew 1:1.

Perhaps the more popular way of understanding this backstory is represented by the well-known aphorism, "The Old Testament is the New Testament concealed and the New Testament is the Old Testament revealed." Though the Hebrew Scriptures prophetically anticipate the Messiah, if we understand the Hebrew Scriptures only as a code concealing God's plan of salvation in Yeshua, then Israel's relationship with God is only a backdrop for the real story - God's plan of redemption in Jesus Christ. Israel's story is then understood as the outworking of the prophesy of the conquering seed of the woman from Genesis 3:15 throughout the Patriarchs' and Israel's history, to the anticipated arrival of "The Seed of the Woman" with the birth of Yeshua.

The difficulty with this traditional view is that the language of the Hebrew Scriptures in no way suggests that Israel is just the backdrop for the real story. Even those passages that predict the coming of Messiah portray the Messiah as the king, deliverer and vindicator of Israel.

Further, God's fidelity to Israel is a defining theme throughout the Hebrew Scriptures. As Isaiah observed, even if a mother could go against every maternal value and forsake the nursing baby at her breast, even if she could do such an abhorrent thing, the God of Israel would never forsake Israel (Isa. 49: 15).

The New Testament Scriptures also portray God's fidelity to Israel through the Messiah. The angel Gabriel declares to Miriam (Mary):

"And behold, you will conceive in your womb and bear a son, and you shall call his name Jesus. He will be great and will be called the Son of the Most High. And the Lord God will give to him the throne of his father David, and he will reign over the house of Jacob forever, and of his kingdom there will be no end." (Luke 1:31–33)

36

Yeshua, the saviour of the world sits on David's throne and *"will reign over the house of Jacob forever."* Luke clearly understood Yeshua to maintain an eternal relationship to the Jewish people as their sovereign ruler, fulfilling the promise to David that his dynasty would endure forever (2 Sam. 7:13; 1 Chron. 17:12). All four gospels record the indictment on Yeshua's cross, the offence for which He was punished to read, "King of the Jews."[17] Even in Yeshua's priestly intercession as the saviour of the world he maintained his deep connection to the Jewish people, dying on the cross as Israel's king (We will discuss the significance of Israel's king dying on behalf of the world in chapter 9, "The King is a Priest.")

The seed of the woman who was to come would defeat the serpent. The image of Genesis 3:15 is this person with his foot on the serpent's head. To place one's foot on the head of another is the picture of a conqueror triumphing over his enemy. Joshua demonstrated Israel's triumph and authority over the kings of Canaan by having his soldiers place their feet on the necks of the defeated kings (Josh. 10:24). Psalm 8:6 observed that God has bestowed authority on humanity over creation, *"You have given him dominion over the works of your hands; you have put all things under his feet."* In the New Testament, this image is applied to the ascended Messiah, seated in authority at God's right hand with *"all things under his feet"* (Eph. 1:22). The seed of the woman is an anticipated ruler who will gain authority over the Serpent, crushing him under his feet.

Genesis continues this theme of the ruler who is to come with the story of Abraham. Beginning with Abraham the promise of a coming ruler is anticipated in Abraham and his descendants. In Genesis 12:2, Abraham is promised a great name. A great name is a hallmark of a king (See, 2 Sam. 7:9), but Abraham and his sons were strangers in a land not their own. Abraham and his sons conversed with kings; they even made treaties with kings. One could say, especially of Abraham,

---

[17] Matt. 27:37; Mark 15:26; Luke 23:38; John 19:19

that he displayed kingly qualities, but he lacked the essential requirement of all kings - a domain over which to rule. Joseph was a ruler, but as a governor on behalf of Pharaoh. Of all the patriarchs, only Joseph ruled over a domain but still he was not the sovereign of Egypt, he still answered to Pharaoh and ruled in his name. Within the covenant God made with Abraham is the promise, *"kings shall come from you"* (Gen. 17:6). This same promise is repeated for Sarah (Gen. 17:16), and later to Jacob (Gen. 35:11).

The promise to Abraham is for a line of kings from his progeny. In Genesis 17, Abraham pleaded with God on behalf of his firstborn, Ishmael (Gen. 17:18). It is significant that the promise of kings was repeated for Sarah and later, to Jacob as well but was not given to Ishmael.[18] Ishmael's descendants did not become kings, but because the promise was made to both Abraham and Sarah it is clear that the line of kings would come not through Ishmael but through Isaac. Isaac's eldest son, Esau did have kings come through his line, even before there were any kings in his younger brother Jacob's line (Gen. 36:31). The promise made to Jacob, *"kings shall come from your own body"* (Gen. 35:11), narrowed the divine election for the coming of *"the seed of the woman"* to the chosen seed of Abraham, his son Isaac and his grandson Jacob.

The central component of the Abrahamic covenant is that through Abraham *"all the families of the earth shall be blessed"* (Gen. 12:3). In Genesis 22:18, the promise is reiterated to clarify that, *"in your offspring shall all the nations of the earth be blessed."* The blessing was to come through Abraham's descendants.

The promise of a line of kings is also included within the Abrahamic covenant. These two themes - that kings will come through the line of the patriarchs, and that through them all the nations will be blessed are not connected in the Genesis narrative. The scriptures will later link the promise of a king(s)

---

[18] God promised Abraham that Ishmael would become a great nation and father 12 princes (Gen. 17:20).

to the promise of the blessing to all the nations, revealing that the blessings to all nations will come through Abraham's descendant, Israel's king.

In Genesis 49, the passage that records Jacob's prophesies over his sons, Jacob asked his children to gather around his bedside so that he might tell them *"what shall happen to [them] in days to come"* (Gen. 49:1). Beginning with the eldest (Reuben), Jacob prophecies the destinies of each son in descending birth order. Joseph is highly favoured of his father and despite his rank as second to last-born, he receives the birthright, a double portion inheritance through Jacob's adoption of Joseph's sons, Ephraim and Manasseh (Gen. 48:5).

Never the less, the rulership did not pass to Joseph but to the fourth born, Judah. [19] Judah's three older brothers were disqualified because of their transgressions against Jacob: Reuben for sleeping with Jacob's concubine, Bilhah (Gen. 35:22; 49:4), and Simeon and Levi for their deceptive and violent revenge against the men of Shechem, because the prince of the city had raped their sister Dinah [20] (Gen. 34:13-27; 49:6,7).

Despite his own moral failures (Gen. 38:12-26), Judah was not disqualified like his three older brothers and was proclaimed as the ruler over all his brothers (Gen. 49:8). Judah was declared as a lion crouched over his prey, daring any to challenge him (Gen. 49:9). [21]

The next line in Jacob's prophesy (Gen. 49:10), clearly stated that rulership belongs to Judah. The Hebrew here is very difficult, particularly the Hebrew word שׁילה (shee-lo´). I have included three representative translations giving the range of meaning for this phrase.

---

[19] 1 Chronicles 5:2 notes the distinction between Judah being the ruler and Joseph receiving the birthright.

[20] Perhaps this was an especially grievous offence because the deception was foisted on the Shechemites by a ruse using circumcision, the sign of the covenant. The brothers profaned the sign that set them apart as holy.

[21] I have had the privilege of seeing lions in the wild. They possess a singular self-confidence and fear no others.

*"The sceptre shall not depart from Judah, nor the ruler's staff from between his feet, until **tribute comes to him**[22] and to him shall be the obedience of the peoples."*
(Gen. 49:10 ESV)

*"The sceptre will not depart from Judah, nor the ruler's staff from between his feet, until **he to whom it belongs** shall come and the obedience of the nations shall be his."*
(Gen. 49:10 NIV)

*"The sceptre shall not depart from Judah, nor a lawgiver from between his feet, until **Shiloh**[23] comes; and to Him shall be the obedience of the people."* (Gen. 49:10 NKJV)

All three representative translations have their merits and their difficulties too. The grammatical criticism of the text is beyond the purview of this book, but even if one sets aside the meaning of the word shee-lo´, the prophecy still speaks of a ruler who is to come from the tribe of Judah, a ruler to whom all peoples owe obedience.

With the curse on the serpent, God promised a ruler who would triumph over the serpent, regaining the authority humanity lost through their yielding to the serpent. Later, Abraham was chosen as the father of the line through whom all nations would be blessed. Abraham is not a king but is promised that kings would come through his line. Jacob prophesied that these kings would come through the line of his son Judah. Particularly, one is coming to whom all peoples owe obedient allegiance.

---

[22] The LXX translates the phrase in a similar fashion to the ESV.
[23] The KJV/NKJV translate the word as a proper name. All references to the town of Shiloh are spelled differently than the word used in Gen. 49:10. In Hebrew, the spelling for the town "Shiloh" omits the Hebrew letter י "yud" (that is שלה not, שׁילה) i.e. Josh.18:1; Judg. 18:31; 1 Sam. 1:3. This does not prove that a proper noun is not in view, though in context, obviously not the town of Shiloh.

40

The promise of the seed of the woman bruising the serpent's head is usually cast in terms of Messiah's redemption. The seed of the woman triumphs over the serpent to bring salvation but in the process is bruised, or wounded himself. Jacob's prophecy over his son Judah added further revelation concerning the identity of the *"seed of the woman."* One can now deduce that the ruler will come from the seed of Judah. Jacob's prophecy to Judah does not focus on redemption. The prophecy highlights all peoples' required obedience to this ruler who is to come. All people pledging obedience to this ruler signifies that in this ruler, the dominion over the planet is actualized once again. The authority to rule over the earth is restored but within a singular ruler over all nations.

The thrust of this book is to highlight the Messiah's identity as God's ruler, and to consider the implications of this identity with respect to creation, the nations and the last days. This is not to discount Yeshua's identity as redeemer/saviour – he is a priest forever, and the king whose reign will never end. Most of us look to Messiah as our saviour before we acknowledge him as our ruler. Of course, there is very good reason for this - without his salvation we could not even begin to comprehend our Messiah or his rule.

Yeshua is forever the crucified one who purchased us for God with his own blood. However, in the overarching purpose of God, Yeshua is the one who restores humanity's rule over planet earth. His identity as saviour is towards this ultimate goal. Yeshua is God's appointed king to rule over creation. He gave his life as a redemptive sacrifice in order to accomplish this purpose as a man, the representative head of the human race.

CHAPTER 4

The Process and Significance of Choosing

The Choosing of Abraham

The ruler who was to come is first described in the most generic sense possible, that is, as the seed of the woman. Eve herself is described as *"the mother of all living"* (Gen. 3:20). In this description there is no choosing of the one over another, from the mother of all will come an offspring chosen to triumph over the serpent. Many generations pass and some of Eve's offspring do well and others do evil. Eventually evil permeates all antediluvian culture and only Noah and his family are spared. We read in the scriptures that Noah *"found favour in the eyes of the LORD"* (Gen. 6:8). He and his family were chosen to survive as a remnant to preserve the human race. The Noah story only hints back to the Genesis 3:15 promise of the triumphant seed of the woman.[24] As discussed in the last chapter, it is not until Abraham's choosing that the focus shifts back to kingship.

Abraham was chosen not only as a godly remnant in a pagan world. He was chosen as the recipient of blessing to disseminate blessings to *"all the families of the earth"* (Gen. 12:3). Abraham was chosen on behalf of others. This choosing of the one for the sake of others continued on through the scriptures as the precedent for chosenness and blessing. Like Noah, Abraham found grace in the eyes of the LORD, but this grace is extended to Abraham on behalf

---

[24] Genesis 9:7 repeats the creation mandate to bear offspring and fill the earth. In the same passage God declares He is establishing His covenant with Noah (Gen. 9:9). Later, Noah blessed the LORD as "the God of Shem" (Gen. 9:26). This suggests a choosing of Shem over his brothers.

43

of others. Abraham is blessed, Abraham will inherit riches, he will have a great name and influence among kings and leaders but ultimately, this is for the sake of all the families of the earth.

This pattern of receiving blessing to be a blessing, first established in Abraham, extends through Israel's relationship to the nations. The blessing to all nations in Abraham passes on through his descendants, the children of Israel. Throughout the scriptures there is the interplay of Israel and the nations.

Like Israel to follow, Abraham was not chosen out of a divine favouritism, but in accordance with God's purposes for the whole world. Abraham was not the ruling seed of the woman who was to come, but in a sense he resembles the ruler. Much like kings, Abraham was blessed and was promised a great name (Gen. 12:2). Though not a king himself, he was promised that kings would come from his line (Gen. 17:6), like the seed of the woman yet to come his choosing was for universal benefit.

Abraham treated with kings as their equal. After defeating a confederacy of Mesopotamian kings, he discussed terms for the distribution of booty with the Canaanite kings that had previously been defeated by those same Mesopotamian rulers (Gen. 14:21). Abraham is sought out by the Philistine king and his commanding general to swear a covenant of friendship (Gen. 21:22,23). When Abraham negotiated the purchase of a tomb for Sarah, the Hittite rulers testified, *"my lord; you are a prince of God among us"* (Gen. 23:6). But unlike the kings he encountered in Canaan, Abraham lacked the primary hallmarks of kingship. To truly be a king one must have a domain to rule within, and subjects to rule over. Though he never received these in his lifetime, Abraham was promised both of these kingly elements by covenant with God.

The central promises of the Abrahamic covenant as they relate to Abraham's own prosperity is the promise of land and descendants. The promise of a myriad of descendants and possession of the land of Canaan are repeated to Abraham more than any other promises contained in the Abrahamic covenant.[25]

---

[25] See, Gen. 12:7; 13:15,17; 15:5,7,18; 17:7,8; 22:17

This emphasis on descendants and land locates the covenant promises squarely with in the material world.

The promise of land is a subject of contention within Christian theology. Some understand the New Covenant to remove the land promise contained in the Abrahamic covenant, emphasizing the spiritual dimensions of the covenant. Paul certainly emphasized the spiritual dimensions of the Abrahamic covenant. He wrote to the Galatians that Yeshua's sacrificial death redeemed all mankind from the curse contained in Torah, *"so that in Christ Jesus the blessing of Abraham might come to the Gentiles, so that we might receive the promised Spirit through faith"* (Gal. 3:14). Paul's reference to God's covenant with Abraham is not an expansion of the promise of land to Gentile believers, nor does it remove the promise of land made to Abraham's descendants. It is the promise of justification by faith as evidenced by the reception of the Holy Spirit.[26]

The Galatians were Gentile Christians who had been deceived into believing they were required to enter God's family through Torah observance. In the letter to the Galatians, Paul emphasised the blessing that was to flow through Abraham to all the families of the earth according to the promise Abraham received by faith. Through the death and resurrection of Messiah Yeshua, and by faith in him, the Galatian believers had appropriated this promise. However, throughout the Hebrew Scriptures there is the expectation of the promise of land for Abraham's descendants. The Scriptures present Israel restored in their own land as an integral dimension of the consummation of all things.

It is beyond the scope of this book to completely settle this contention. The dichotomy between the material and spiritual world is not a required choice of one over the other. The anticipated consummation of all things is the will of God now done in heaven also done on earth (Matt. 6:10). It is the glory of

---

[26] Ronald Y.K. Fung, "The Epistle to the Galatians." NICNT. Editor, F.F. Bruce. (Grand Rapids, MI: Eerdmans, 1988) 152,153.

God that now fills all of heaven also filling all the earth (Hab. 2:14). Even within many Christian theologies of the kingdom there is both a spiritual and material dimension.[27] The promise of land to Abraham's descendants roots the plan of God squarely within the created world.

Jewish theologian, Michael Wyschogrod explained, "the circumcised body of Israel is the dark, carnal presence through which the redemption makes its way into history."[28] This may seem strange to Christian ears - most of us would associate "carnal" with Paul's rebuke to the Corinthian church (1 Cor. 3:1). Wyschogrod is using the term in a more literal sense. God is Spirit; the single most tangible evidence of God's activity within the material world is the enduring presence of Israel.

Wyschogrod contends that salvation history moves within the material world through the body of Israel. Israel is "the carnal anchor that God has sunk into the soil of creation."[29] Further, God's relation to humanity "flows through his relation to Israel."[30] Wyschogrod is an Orthodox Jew, for him there is no Israel receding into the background with the birth of Yeshua. Wyschogrod does a great service to all Christians by challenging us to consider the role of Israel within the plan for creation's consummation.

One cannot seriously consider Israel in the biblical sense apart from the land of Israel. The promise of descendants and land go together. Both Abraham's and Israel's choosing demonstrate that God's love for the world moves beyond concepts and philosophy. God's activity and His love connect within space and time with specific individuals in specific domains.

---

[27] G. Goldsworthy, "Kingdom of God." New Dictionary of Biblical Theology (IVP-Biblical Theology) © 2000 by Inter-Varsity Press. Electronic text hypertexted and prepared by OakTree Software, Inc. Version 2.2. 616-619.

[28] Michael Wyschogrod, "The Body of Faith." (Lanham, MD: Rowan & Littlefield, 1983) 256.

[29] Ibid.

[30] Ibid. 102.

To say that God is love without that love connecting to specific objects of that love, reduces love to a vague notion. The ultimate demonstration of God's love within the material world is "*the Word made flesh*" dwelling among us. As we will later explore, the Lord from heaven made flesh is inextricably connected to the House of Jacob and the land of Israel.

If one understands Yeshua to be Israel's eternal king, the role of Israel within the canonical narrative endures. It is through Israel, and specifically, through Israel's king that the proper order of authority is re-established within creation. The ruler who crushes the serpent's head is the king who comes through the line of Judah. His domain expands beyond the borders of Canaan and beyond the family of Israel to all peoples and all nations. Israel does not fade into insignificance because in the material world, Israel is the "carnal presence through which the redemption makes its way into history."[31]

The Choosing of the Nation

When God chose Israel as His "*treasured possession among all peoples*" (Exod. 19:5), He demonstrated the relationship He established between Israel, Israel's king and the nations. With Israel's choosing, Abraham's family line election expanded onto a national scale. Israel was set apart from all other "peoples" as a unique and exceedingly valuable "possession" within God's sovereign choosing. The grounds for this election were God's ownership and authority as the Creator. The earth belongs to God, and therefore He has the sovereign right to choose any facet of His created order for His own purpose. The nation of Israel at the time of this choosing was hardly a nation in the conventional sense. They had been slaves with no status, no domain within to govern, or any national self-determination for 400 years.

There is an irony to addressing such a rag-tag nation as God's treasured possession among all. In a sense, Israel's status at the time of her choosing was only a latent possibility. The promise

---

[31] Wyschogrod, "The Body of Faith" 256.

was conditional on Israel obeying God's voice and keeping His covenant (Exod. 19:5). The Creator chose the least of all nations (Deut. 7:7), a nation of slaves for His purpose.

By entering into covenant with Israel He transformed them from the lowest nation, to the nation above all. Exodus 19:6 explained that this purpose is redemptive. Israel was described as *"a kingdom of priests and a holy nation."* Israel as the *"holy nation"* was a reiteration of Israel as the chosen people "among all peoples" promised in Exodus 19:5. Israel is holy, that is, set apart, or chosen for God's purposes. Israel as *"a kingdom of priests"* describes the function of the chosen nation and its governmental structure.

All priesthoods function as intermediaries between the people and the divine. A priest represents the people to God and God to the people. Within Israel's national structure, Aaron and his sons were ordained as priests to represent Israel to God and God to Israel. Exodus 19:6 ordained the whole nation as a priesthood to represent all the nations to God and God to all nations.

Israel as a priesthood was organized as a kingdom. How national priesthood and kingdom go together is not clear within the Exodus 19 passage. At the time of the exodus, Israel's monarchy was still some 400 years into the future. The Torah assigns great authority to the High Priest. During the wilderness wanderings Aaron and Moses functioned both as priests over the nation and as national rulers. Following settlement within the Promised Land, the High Priest was given Supreme Court authority to judge over legal disputes (Deut. 17:8-11). The duration of exile for one guilty of manslaughter within a city of refuge, was determined by the life span of the presiding High Priest (Num. 35:28). The required sin offering for the presiding High Priest was a bull (Lev. 4:3) - the equivalent offering required of the whole nation (Lev. 4:13).

The offering requirements listed in Leviticus 4 do not include an offering for a king, only the offering for a leader.[32] This

---

[32] The meaning of the Hebrew "nāś'i" (נשׂיא), is never understood to mean king and is usually translated as prince, chief or leader.

offering was a male goat (Lev. 4:22), a less substantial offering than the bull required for the High Priest. Taken together these Torah statutes suggest that Israel was to be a pure theocracy. God Himself was to be Israel's king and the High Priest; God's representative among the people was to rule as His regent. The later story of King Saul's coronation (I Sam. 8:7) seems to support this view.

In as much as the Torah highlights the authority of the High Priest, the Torah also anticipates a king who will rule over Israel. [33] As we have already covered in the Genesis passages (especially Genesis 49:10), a king was to come from the line of Judah. As the writer of Hebrews observed, *"in connection with that tribe Moses said nothing about priests"* (Heb. 7:14).

The Balaam oracles within the book of Numbers provide significant information regarding Israel's king that support Jacob's prophesy in Genesis 49. Balaam was hired by the king of Moab to curse Israel. Despite his spurious character, the words Balaam spoke were the oracles of God (Num. 23:5,15; 24:2, Deut. 23:4; Jos. 24:9). Balaam's first oracle identified Israel as God's unique nation, set apart for divine purpose:

"For from the top of the crags I see him, from the hills I behold him; behold, a people dwelling alone, and not counting itself among the nations!" (Num. 23:9)

The fact that Israel was separate from the nations supports Israel's identity as a priesthood on behalf of the nations, and sets the paradigm for Israel's function within God's purposes of redemption and consummation. From the divine perspective the world is divided into two distinct groups, Israel and the nations.

---

[33] Many commentators have explained the Torah's seeming contradiction between the priest ruler and the anticipated king ruler by assigning separate traditions to the formation of the Torah - what is commonly known as the Documentary Hypothesis. It is not within my purview to comment on the merits and limitations of the Documentary Hypothesis. However, in my opinion the Torah emphasizes both because God's ruler is both a king and a priest.

Israel and the nations are set in a relationship of mutual blessing together for God's purposes. Israel was set aside in Exodus 19 to function as priests on behalf of the nations.

In the New Testament, Paul made the startling claim that the nations received salvation in order to make Israel jealous (Rom. 11:11). In a similar relationship, Abraham was blessed in order for the nations to be blessed (Gen. 12:3).[34]

This theme of Israel and the nations continues throughout the scriptures. Even in the consummation, the nations enter New Jerusalem through gates inscribed with the names of Israel's 12 sons (Rev. 21:12, 24-26). As we shall observe below, Balaam's oracles speak of Israel's king. As befitting a nation distinct from all others, so too Israel's king was to be unique to all other kings. As Israel is a nation set apart for all nations, so too the rule of Israel's king is for the sake of all nations.

Balaam's second oracle speaks directly about Israel's king:

> *"The LORD their God is with them, and the shout of a king is among them. God brings them out of Egypt and is for them like the horns of a wild ox... 'Behold, a people! As a lioness it rises up and as a lion it lifts itself; it does not lie down until it has devoured the prey and drunk the blood of the slain.'"* (Num. 23:21,24)

This first reference to kingship in Balaam's oracles could support the idea that God Himself is Israel's king. The prophecy compares God delivering Israel *"like the horns of a wild ox."* Horns and particularly the horns of the wild ox (Hebrew, *ra͞'am* [ראם]), signify majesty.[35] The next image, the lion/lioness triumphant over its prey hearkens back to Jacob's prophecy over Judah *"crouched as a lion and as a lioness"* over its prey (Gen. 49:9,10).

---

[34] For further comment on the interplay between Israel and the nations see, Shoub, "To the Jew First" 55-70.
[35] See, Deut. 33:17; Ps. 92:10

This section of the oracle begins with acclaiming God as Israel's deliverer from Egyptian bondage: "*The LORD their God is with them.*" How are we to understand the second line in this stanza? Is "*the shout of the king*" among them simply synonymous parallelism? Perhaps, especially because God is the one who "*brings them out of Egypt.*" However, the remaining third and fourth oracles provide further information, revealing that the "*shout of the king*" indicates that a representative king is in view.

Balaam's third oracle speaks of an exalted king coming out of Egypt:

> "*His king shall be higher than Agag, and his kingdom shall be exalted. God brings him out of Egypt and is for him like the horns of the wild ox; he shall eat up the nations, his adversaries, and shall break their bones in pieces and pierce them through with his arrows. He crouched, he lay down like a lion and like a lioness; who will rouse him up?*" (Num. 24:7–9)

The third oracle's king reference is similar to the description in the second oracle, but here, not only is "*the shout of the king*" among them but a specific king is mentioned. In Balaam's second oracle (Num. 23:22), God brings "*them*" out of Egypt. In Balaam's third oracle (Num. 24:8), God brings "*Him*" out of Egypt.[36] In this third oracle, it is Israel's king brought out of Egypt with the nation, that is crouching as a lion reminiscent of Genesis 49:9.

Balaam's fourth oracle provides even further information about the king. In this oracle the reference is to a future king to come:

---

[36] Martin Pickup, "New Testament Interpretation of the Old Testament: The Theological Rationale of Midrashic Exegesis" JETS 51/2 (June 2008): 371-378. Pickup observed that early Jewish commentators applied midrashic exegesis to Balaam's oracles, interpreting them with the understanding that a messianic king was in view. The LXX translation of Numbers 24:7,8 supports Pickup's view.

"I see him, but not now; I behold him, but not near: a star shall come out of Jacob, and a scepter shall rise out of Israel... his enemies, shall be dispossessed. Israel is doing valiantly. And one from Jacob shall exercise dominion and destroy the survivors of cities!" (Num. 24:17–19)

Balaam sees this king afar off, he is *"not now...not near."* In Balaam's second oracle *"the shout of the king"* is with Israel. In the third oracle, God brings this king *"out of Egypt"* with the children of Israel, but in this last oracle, this king is yet to come, *"one from Jacob shall exercise dominion."*[37]

The king who will exercise dominion, the lion that crouches over his prey and subdues nations came out of Egypt with Israel and is also yet to come. This "now and not yet" dimension of kingly presence among Israel is a difficult concept, but is consistent with the Apostolic witness to the Exodus. As Paul commented to the Corinthians regarding Israel's wilderness wanderings, *"and all drank the same spiritual drink. For they drank from the spiritual Rock that followed them, and the Rock was Christ"* (1 Cor. 10:4).

Balaam's oracles were inspired blessings upon the nation not reckoned among other nations, a nation standing alone, chosen by God. God is their king, ruling among them and yet there is an appointed king who mysteriously travels among them and is also still to come. Balaam referenced the imagery of a lion standing over his prey, first employed by Jacob to speak of a future king who would come from the line of Judah, to whom all nations owe allegiance and obedience. Both Jacob and Balaam referenced a king of Israel yet to come who will have dominion over the nations.

Deuteronomy also makes reference to a king to come. Unlike the prophecies of Jacob and Balaam, Deuteronomy is not concerned with grand themes of awesome majesty and world dominion. Deuteronomy gives practical instructions for the king to come. These instructions reflect the original kingly mandate given

---

[37] Hebrew, rādāh (רדה) is the same word used in the original creation mandate (Gen. 1:28).

to Adam at the beginning of the age. Adam was to rule under God's authority, he was to be completely reliant on God for his capacity to rule and make wise decisions; so too, Israel's king. The one to whom *"shall be the obedience of the peoples"* (Gen. 49:10), and *"shall exercise dominion and destroy the survivor of cities"* (Num. 24:19), was required to exercise authority in his kingdom contrary to the characteristics of all other rulers.

Deuteronomy 17:14-20 outlines the instructions for a ruler in Israel. The first stipulations are that the king is to be chosen by God and must be a native born Israeli. One would expect these requirements but in addition, there are three prohibitions one would not expect for a ruler:

A. He is not to acquire many horses (Deut. 17:16)
B. He is not to acquire many wives (Deut. 17:17)
C. He is not to acquire large amounts of
   gold and silver (Deut. 17:17)

Horses, wives and gold are obvious signs of wealth and prestige but for rulers they were practical necessities. Horses were not just a status symbol corresponding to modern day luxury cars. A horse was more so the equivalent of a modern day fighter jet or armored tank. A horse represented state of the art military technology. Horses pulled chariots and carried mounted cavalry into battle. A ruler needed horses to ensure military prowess.

Many wives were not primarily to satisfy the lusts of the king. Many wives meant many sons. Sons were necessary to ensure the continuation of the dynasty, and to fill key administrative roles as trusted members of the king's political circle.

Gold and silver were necessary for rulers in the ancient world for the same reason financial wealth is necessary for contemporary political success. The three elements necessary for a successful rule in ancient times were prohibited to Israel's king. The success of his kingdom was not to be based on standard operating procedures. The king of Israel's success was based on his dependence and reliance on the ultimate king of Israel, under whom he was to rule as a regent:

"And when he sits on the throne of his kingdom, he shall write for himself in a book a copy of this law, approved by the Levitical priests. And it shall be with him, and he shall read in it all the days of his life, that he may learn to fear the LORD his God by keeping all the words of this law and these statutes, and doing them, that his heart may not be lifted up above his brothers, and that he may not turn aside from the commandment, either to the right hand or to the left, so that he may continue long in his kingdom, he and his children, in Israel." (Deut. 17:18–20)

The king was to write out his own copy of the Torah and *"read it all the days of his life,"* in order to ensure that his judgments and ruling decisions would comply with the statues and commandments of God. The king was not to rule according to what he determined was good and evil, but according to the pattern originally set out for humanity, according to what God had determined to be good and evil. The king was to be a man *"under authority."* The king was to be a counter-king to all other rulers. Submission to God, not power, influence and wealth was the assurance of the king's success and duration.

From the beginning God had set a pattern within the created order for mankind to rule over creation. During the wilderness wanderings the priests, as God's representatives to the people, were the ruling authority over the nation. Within the Torah there is the prophetic anticipation of a king and even specific instructions for how the king would rule over the nation, once they entered into the promised land.

Joshua was chosen as the leader of Israel for the conquest of Canaan. Joshua was not crowned king, he was appointed as Israel's leader through ordination by Moses (Deut. 34:9). Joshua was given instructions to rule that follow the prescription for the kings who were to come. Joshua was not required to write his own copy of the Torah, but like the king to come he was to immerse himself in Torah. The king to come was *"not to turn aside from the commandment, either to the right hand or the left, so that he may continue long in his kingdom"* (Deut. 17:20). Joshua personally received similar instructions from the God of Israel:

> *"Only be strong and courageous, being careful to do according to all the law that Moses my servant commanded you. Do not turn from it to the right hand or to the left, that you may have good success wherever you go. This Book of the Law shall not depart from your mouth, but you shall meditate on it day and night, so that you may be careful to do according to all that is written in it. For then you will make your way prosperous, and then you will have good success."* (Jos. 1:7–8)

Like the king that was to come, Joshua was to rule under God's authority. His success was predicated on his submission to God's instructions. Only by being *"careful to do all that is written"* in the Torah would he have success as Israel's leader. Again, this follows the pattern God set for humanity's rule at creation.

In a sense, Israel was to become God's representative ruler on earth. Israel did not yet have ruling authority over the nations, but as God's chosen nation they were to follow His authority paradigm. Even Israel's chosenness was predicated on the nation submitting to God's instructions (Exod. 19:5). By submitting to God's authority, Israel would ascend to become the greatest of all nations. Israel would become *"the head [nation] and not the tail"* (Deut. 28:13), lending to many nations and borrowing from none (Deut. 28:12), surpassing all other nations in prosperity and military might. As a result, all other nations would acknowledge Israel's chosen status and would fear her (Deut. 28:2-10).

Between the death of Joshua and the beginning of kingdom rule in Israel was the period of the Judges. [38] Like the later chronologies of Israel's kings, the book of Judges presents a chronological order to the duration of each judge's rule. But these

---

[38] This interim was of significant duration similar in scope to the monarchy (around 400 years). Exact time frames are disputed.

rulers were not equivalent to monarchs. Their domain was usually localized to a specific region within the confederation of tribes.[39]

Even those judges who had national authority, likely did not provide national governance equivalent to monarchs, but were called upon to settle difficult disputes (Deut. 17:9), or to lead a tribe or confederation of tribes in battle against an enemy. The era of the judges is marked by apostasy and disobedience. As the book of Judges draws to a close, the author provides editorial comment on the nation's moral, social, spiritual and political failures by noting Israel's precarious government authority.

> *"In those days there was no king in Israel. Everyone did what was right in his own eyes."* (Judges 17:6)[40]

Because Israel had no central monarch to govern over the people, the rule of law was not enforced within the nation. The king was to rule according to the commandments of Torah. Without a king, each individual took it upon himself/herself to be the final adjudicator of what was good and what was evil. As we noted in the early chapters of Genesis, individual self-determination of good and evil was one of the most significant consequences of the fall.

According to Deuteronomy 17:14-20, the Torah set out expectations and instructions for kings to rule in Israel. For almost 400 years judges had ruled in Israel. The author of the book of Judges, commenting on the moral lapse within Israeli society during this time period noted that everyone determined what was right in their own eyes because, *"In those days there was no king."* Therefore, it is curious that in 1 Samuel, the book that transitions from the rule of judges to the rule of kings, the initial request for a king is met with divine disapproval.

---

[39] Barry G. Webb, "Judges." New Bible Commentary (IVP-NB Commentary). Editors: D.A. Darson, R.T. France. J.A. Motyer, G.J. Wenham (Downers Grove, IL: IVP, 1994) 261.

[40] See also, Judges 18:1; 19:1; 21:25

Israel's elders approached Samuel to appoint a king over the people. Their request was based (at least in part), on their lack of confidence in Samuel's successors, his sons Joel and Abijah:

> *"Then all the elders of Israel gathered together and came to Samuel at Ramah and said to him, 'Behold, you are old and your sons do not walk in your ways. Now appoint for us a king to judge us like all the nations.' But the thing displeased Samuel when they said, 'Give us a king to judge us.' And Samuel prayed to the LORD. And the LORD said to Samuel, 'Obey the voice of the people in all that they say to you, for they have not rejected you, but they have rejected me from being king over them.'"*
> (1 Sam. 8:4–7)

As we have been tracking throughout this chapter, the Torah anticipated a king to come from Genesis through Deuteronomy. The Samuel passage provides some clues as to why this seemingly legitimate request, anticipated in Torah was displeasing both to Samuel and to God. Israel's elders requested a king *"to judge us like all the nations."* Even the Deuteronomy 17 text employs a similar phrase, *"When you come to the land that the LORD your God is giving you, and you possess it and dwell in it and then say, 'I will set a king over me, like all the nations that are around me'"* (Deut. 17:14).

The difference between the phrases is telling. The Deuteronomy passage acknowledges that Israel, like all the nations around her will one day request a king. The 1 Samuel passage is a request for a king to judge Israel in the same fashion as the kingdoms around her.

This is further borne out by Samuel's description of the king Israel had requested. Unlike the anticipated king of Deuteronomy, this king will amass horses and chariots (1 Sam. 8:11) and he will acquire wealth through unscrupulous taxation (1 Sam. 8: 14-17). Samuel's description of the king to come does not mention taking many wives but the future scenario of Israel under the king of their own choosing anticipates Israel being enslaved to this king, *"He will take the tenth of your flocks, and you shall be his slaves"*

(1 Sam. 8:17). The king anticipated in Deuteronomy 17 was to rule according to the commands of Torah so *that his heart may not be lifted up above his brothers.*" Clearly, the king Israel was requesting was not the king described in Deuteronomy 17. Even after Samuel described for them the type of king they desired, that he would enslave them and rule over them without regard for their welfare they still answered Samuel:

> *"No! But there shall be a king over us, that we also may be like all the nations, and that our king may judge us and go out before us and fight our battles."* (1 Sam. 8:19–20)

Israel that had been set apart from all other nations wanted to be *"like all the other nations."* Beginning with Saul son of Kish, until the destruction of the kingdom of Judah by the Babylonians some 400 years later, all of Israel and Judah's monarchs failed to live up to the standard set out in Deuteronomy 17. But of all the kings of Israel and Judah, it is David, the man after God's own heart who is held up as the template for the king to come, the king who would obey the LORD's commands completely.

The Choosing of a Man

Israel had asked for a king in order to be like all the nations that surrounded her. This displeased the LORD because this was contrary to the template set out for Israel's king in Deuteronomy 17. Israel's king was to be different from the kings of all other nations. The LORD granted Israel's request and Saul son of Kish became Israel's first king. As Samuel had warned the elders of Israel, Saul's leadership did not bless the nation nor did it fulfill God's expectation for Israel's king.

The chief quality of Israel's king was to be his obedience to God's commands. The king was required to write out his own scroll of the Torah and read it *"all the days of his life, that he may learn to fear the LORD his God by keeping all the words of this law"* (Deut. 17:19). Saul's reign was characterized by his disobedience.

Saul was rejected as king because he failed to obey God's instructions. Samuel rebuked Saul for his disobedience:

> *"And Samuel said, "Has the LORD as great delight in burnt offerings and sacrifices, as in obeying the voice of the LORD? Behold, to obey is better than sacrifice, and to listen than the fat of rams… Because you have rejected the word of the LORD, he has also rejected you from being king."* (1 Sam. 15:22–23)

Samuel was directed by God to anoint another to replace Saul. God's choice was unexpected. Even Samuel, acquainted with the ways of God was surprised by God's choice of David, the youngest and outwardly least kingly of Jesse's seven sons. The Holy Spirit reminded Samuel *"man looks on the outward appearance, but the LORD looks on the heart"* (1 Sam. 16:7).

Samuel had told Saul that his kingdom would not continue; rather the LORD had *"Sought out a man after his own heart."* In contrast to disobedient Saul, David, a man after God's own heart would be an obedient king. David is known for many things, his bravery, his passion, his overcoming faith, but despite his shortcomings he was a man after God's own heart because he sought to please God and obey His word.

I think most of us underestimate David's love for the Torah of God. Perhaps foremost in our minds is Yeshua's example of David eating the Showbread, contrary to Torah's instructions (Matt. 12:3,4) and how during David's reign the Ark of the Covenant was housed outside of the Tabernacle, contrary the order prescribed by Torah (1 Chron. 16:1; 2 Chron. 1:3,4).

However, Scripture sets David as the benchmark of obedience for all kings who would come after him. When God reproved Jeroboam through the prophet Ahijah he said: *"you have not been like my servant David, who kept my commandments and followed me with all his heart, doing only that which was right in my eyes"* (1 Kings 14:8).

Further, David's writings also testify to his love for Torah and his desire to follow God's instructions. Psalm 1 serves as a prologue to the Psalter.

The first line of the first Psalm is:

"Blessed is the man who walks not in the counsel of the wicked, nor stands in the way of sinners, nor sits in the seat of scoffers; but his delight is in the law of the LORD, and on his law he meditates day and night." (Ps. 1:1–2)

Psalm 119, David's longest psalm has 25 references to the Torah. The first line serves as the theme verse for the entire Psalm. It echoes Psalm 1:1,2:

"Blessed are those whose way is blameless, who walk in the law of the LORD!" (Ps. 119:1)

David was committed to obeying God's commands. His last words to his successor Solomon were instructions to obey God's commands:

"Now therefore in the sight of all Israel, the assembly of the LORD, and in the hearing of our God, observe and seek out all the commandments of the LORD your God, that you may possess this good land and leave it for an inheritance to your children after you forever." (1 Chron. 28:8)

David the man after God's own heart was not only chosen to rule over the nation of Israel in his generation, but to establish a dynasty that would fulfill the prophetic rulership mandate set out to Adam and the Patriarchs. As we have discussed in previous chapters, it had always been God's intention to appoint a king over Israel to move forward the divine plan to wrest power away from the Serpent back to mankind.

After David had been appointed king and the ark was secured in Jerusalem, David desired to build a temple to house the ark in a permanent location. In response to David's inquiry of the prophet Nathan, the LORD sent David this message:

"Now, therefore, thus you shall say to my servant David, 'Thus says the LORD of hosts… I will make for you a great name, like the name of the great ones of the earth… And I will give you rest from all your enemies. Moreover, the LORD declares to you that the LORD will make you a house. When your days are fulfilled and you lie down with your fathers, I will raise up your offspring after you, who shall come from your body, and I will establish his kingdom. He shall build a house for my name, and I will establish the throne of his kingdom forever. I will be to him a father, and he shall be to me a son. When he commits iniquity, I will discipline him with the rod of men, with the stripes of the sons of men, but my steadfast love will not depart from him, as I took it from Saul, whom I put away from before you. And your house and your kingdom shall be made sure forever before me. Your throne shall be established forever.'"
(2 Sam. 7:8–16)

The key promise of 2 Samuel 7 is an enduring legacy. David would not build a house for the LORD; the LORD would build a house for David. Nathan's prophecy refers to Solomon, who would fulfill David's desire to build a permanent house for the ark, and an expectation that the line would continue through David's offspring. There is some foreshadowing that not all of David's sons would exhibit the same sort of devotion as their father. But even when they were disobedient, God's "steadfast love"[41] would not be removed from David's line as it was from Saul. David's house would *"be established forever."* This enduring legacy is promised to David despite the possibility that his children may not follow his example of obedience and devotion.

---

[41] Hebrew, kheh´-sed (חֶסֶד), does not have a direct English equivalent. It is often translated as mercy, loving kindness, and steadfast love. In the context of divine speech it is best understood as covenant fidelity - divine love and mercy that flows out of covenant relationship (See, Deut. 7:9; Isa. 54:10). Nathan's prophecy is referred to as a covenant in Psalm 89:3,4. Theologians sometimes refer to 2 Samuel 7: 8-16 and the equivalent passage in 1 Chronicles 17:7-14 as the Davidic covenant.

Somehow the promise would be secured, despite the character of David's offspring.

The promise refers to the future Davidic kings as God's son. In Christian parlance, we understand the term "Son of God" to refer to Yeshua, the divine son, the second person of the trinity. Certainly there is an intentional inference from the phrase that foreshadows the divine "SON" of God. But the immediate context defines the term as Israel's king.[42] According to 2 Samuel 7:14, the "son" of God is capable of iniquity – obviously this is not referring to the divine Son. A clear example of how Israel understood the King and the son of God to be synonymous terms is found in John 1:49. In response to Yeshua's recognition of Nathaniel prior to their face-to-face meeting, Nathaniel replied: *"Rabbi, you are the Son of God! You are the King of Israel!"*

In Exodus 4:22, God instructed Moses to inform Pharaoh: *"Thus says the LORD, Israel is my firstborn son, and I say to you, 'Let my son go that he may serve me.'"* Prior to the appointment of her king, Israel the nation as a whole is reckoned as God's son. This familial relationship speaks of a special closeness between Israel and the Creator. Following God's choosing of a kingly line the king represents Israel as God's son.

A son is expected to represent his father. A son is to exhibit the characteristics of his father and within a monarchial system the prince (son), exercises authority on behalf of the king (father). With the advent of the Davidic covenant, the king of Israel is delegated with an authority to represent the supreme King, the God of Israel to the nation. The king of Israel as God's delegated ruler is held to a high level of accountability, and would face punishment for disobedience. The king of Israel also enjoys a special familial relationship with the God of Israel, and is promised God's enduring love and faithfulness.

---

[42] Orthodox Jewish Scholar Daniel Boyarin notes that counter-intuitively, the term "Son of God" refers to Messiah's earthly identity as king and the term "Son of Man" refers to Messiah's divine identity. We will discuss this matter in chapter 6 "The Kings of the Earth." See, Daniel Boyarin. "The Jewish Gospels" (NY, NY: The New Press. 2012) 27-34

This special relationship between the God of Israel and the king of Israel held significant import for the prosperity of the nation. A review of Israel's monarchial history shows a clear pattern: As with king, so with nation. All the kings of Israel and Judah were evaluated according to their obedience to God's commands. When the king obeyed God's commands he did well and the nation was rewarded with God's blessings. When the king disobeyed God's commands he did evil and subsequently, the nation came under judgment. As God's son over the nation of Israel, the king's behavior was the primary factor determining the nation's prosperity. As we shall later explore, Israel's Messiah king will secure Israel's ultimate destiny.

The parallel passage for 2 Samuel 7:8-16 is 1 Chronicles 17:7-14. Chronicles is a much later document, written during the post – exilic period.[43] Within the span of prophetic revelation, the parallel Chronicles passage shifts the expectation from an enduring dynasty for David's line to the enduring reign of one of David's future offspring. The 1 Chronicles passage begins with the same words as the 2 Samuel passage, but the text shifts with respect to God's promise of an enduring house:

> *"Moreover, I declare to you that the LORD will build you a house. When your days are fulfilled to walk with your fathers, I will raise up your offspring after you, one of your own sons, and I will establish his kingdom. He shall build a house for me, and I will establish his throne forever. I will be to him a father, and he shall be to me a son. I will not take my steadfast love from him, as I took it from him who was before you, but I will confirm him in my house and in my kingdom forever, and his throne shall be established forever.'"*
> (1 Chron. 17:10–14)

In 2 Samuel, it is David's throne that endures forever through God's enduring "steadfast love" to David's descendants. The

---

[43] 1 Chronicles 3:17-23 records eight generations of David's line after the Babylonian exile.

passage includes the caveat that should any of these sons prove unfaithful they would be punished (2 Sam. 7:14). In the 1 Chronicles passage, there is no mention of the potential for punishment. The security of David's line is promised through one particular descendant. God promised to *"confirm him in my house and in my kingdom forever."* Moreover, God assured David that this offspring's throne *"shall be established forever* (1 Chron. 17:14).

The expectation for a future king appointed by God began with the fall of mankind from their intended rulership as God's regents over the planet. God promised that a descendent of Eve would come who would crush the Serpent's head, thereby re-establishing the divine order for authority on earth.[44] God chose Abraham and his family as the conduits through which this king would eventually arise. On his deathbed, Jacob prophesied that this king would come through the line of his son Judah.[45]

When God redeemed Israel from slavery, and set them apart as His holy nation, He did so with the expectation that a king would arise out of Jacob who would exercise authority over the nations. According to Balaam's prophecy, this king accompanied Israel out of bondage and yet at the time of the exodus was still anticipated to come at some future date.[46] Before Israel entered the Promised Land, Moses wrote explicit instructions for the king whom God would choose once Israel was established in Canaan. Unlike the kings who ruled over the nations, this king was not to establish his dynasty through military power, nepotism or wealth. The king's security rested on his obedience to God's commands. The king was to *"not to be lifted up above his brothers"* (Deut. 17:20); rather he was to write his own copy of the Torah *"that he may learn to fear the LORD his God by keeping all the words of this law and these statutes"* (Deut. 17:19).

The king was to be an obedient servant, exercising rulership according to God's commandments. The people chose Saul because they wanted a king to rule over them like all the other

---

[44] Genesis 3:15
[45] Genesis 49:10
[46] Numbers 24:8,9 cf. Numbers 24:17-19

kingdoms around them. God acquiesced to their demands but because Saul was not a king according to the criteria of Torah, his kingdom failed.

God replaced Saul with a king after his own heart. David was a king who ruled Israel by serving Israel's God. His obedience was not perfect, but his life demonstrated a fidelity to God and God's commands. God entered into a covenant with David, assuring him that his line would endure forever. As prophetic revelation continued on, a clearer picture emerged of a unique descendant of David whose reign would endure forever.

The term Messiah is a generic Hebrew term for one who has been anointed. In this sense, Israel has had many "messiahs." Over time the term has been reserved for only one: The Davidic king whose rule endures over all forever. The Messiah (God's chosen ruler), is the one promised at the beginning to restore God's rule on earth. Beginning with his incarnation and confirmed through his death and resurrection, we know this promised one is Yeshua of Nazareth, Son of David, Son of Abraham, Son of God.

In the following chapters we will explore how Yeshua's rule extends beyond Israel to all nations, and ultimately ushers in the consummation of all things, restoring the original creation mandate for mankind to have dominion over planet earth.

Part Two

The King of Israel and the Nations

CHAPTER 5

The Mandate to Rule and the Nations

In Genesis 1:28, God bestowed the rulership mandate over the planet to the first couple. Though they represented the entire human race, as just two people their capacity to rule was limited to their function within the Garden of Eden. The intent of the ruling mandate extended far beyond Eden to all the fish in the sea, the birds in the air, and *"over every living thing that moves on the earth."* Humanity's rule represented by the first couple would need to expand through their progeny to the four corners of the globe. That is why the directive to rule is prefaced with the command: *"be fruitful and multiply and fill the earth."*

Genesis 6:1 explained that humanity *"began to multiply on the face of the earth."* The narrative also explained, *"that every intention of the thoughts of his heart was only evil continually"* (Gen. 6:5). Though humanity obeyed the directive to fill the earth, they also filled it with violence. This was a hideous betrayal of the dominion mandate. Mankind's governance on earth was in complete rebellion against the Creator's intentions.

As a consequence, mankind was almost destroyed, *"but Noah found favor in the eyes of the LORD"* (Gen. 6:8). The LORD preserved a remnant in Noah and his family in keeping with His promise to defeat the Serpent through one of Eve's offspring (Gen. 3:15). In a sense, the creation mandate was re-instituted with Noah and his family. However, the terms were different. Noah's mandate begins with the same instructions given to Adam and Eve, *"Be fruitful and multiply and fill the earth"* (Gen. 9:1), but instead of the directive to rule over all the other creatures, now Noah and his family receive the bounty of the earth and everything that moves on it as food for their sustenance.

From henceforth, all the animals that had previously submitted to Adam without fear would be fearful of Noah and the rest of mankind. The relationship with nature had shifted adversarially. One can still control those who are inherently fearful, but one cannot rule over creatures in a way that fulfills the creation mandate when one's subjects dread their ruler.

The generations that followed Noah did not obey the creation mandate to fill the earth. Instead of spreading out across the globe, Noah's descendants settled in the plain of Shinar, in Mesopotamia (Gen. 11:1). Genesis 11 describes the building of the tower of Babel and the subsequent scattering of the nations throughout the earth. Genesis 11 has been described as the genesis of the nations, how humanity went from one people and one language in one place, to many peoples speaking many languages across the globe. From the Genesis 11 narrative one could understand the formation of the nations as a negative consequence to Noah's descendants choosing to *"make a name"* for themselves, in order to prevent their being scattered *"over the face of all the earth"* (Gen. 11:4).

However, the command to fill the earth goes back to the creation mandate. Humanity was never intended to stay in one place but to spread out to the four corners of the globe. It is very probable that in doing so the one language, one culture, human family would have over time developed multiple languages and multiple cultures connected to the different regions of the earth.

God's scattering of the nations by confusing their language hastened a process that I believe would have happened naturally over time. The end result may not have been exactly as it has unfolded since Babel, but just as Swiss German dialects change dramatically from one isolated mountain valley to another, it is very probable that languages would have changed over time even without the Babel incident. This is so because of the vast distances different family groups would have had to travel in their movements as they spread out across the globe.[47]

---

[47] I am not a philologist nor do I pretend to be an expert on language theory. My point is simply that no matter how one understands Genesis 11

A multitude of languages brings glory to God. John's heavenly vision of redeemed humanity worshipping the Lamb and the One who sits on the throne is described as a vast multitude composed of *"every nation, from all tribes and peoples and languages"* (Rev. 7:9).

Paul also bore witness to God's intention to have humanity divide into multiple nations:

"And He has made from one blood every nation of men to dwell on all the face of the earth, and has determined their preappointed times and the boundaries of their dwellings." (Acts 17:26 NKJV)

God is the creator of the nations. He has determined *"their preappointed times,"* that is, their unique role in history to accomplish God's purposes, and *"the boundaries of their dwellings,"* their geographical borders, or their specific area in which to dwell. Paul's statement clears up any confusion[48] regarding the genesis of the nations. The nations were God's idea from the beginning; they are not simply the outcome of God scattering the people at Babel. The incident at Babel is consistent with humanity's trait to determine their own way apart from God's purposes. The divine directive was *"fill the earth,"* the human response was, *"Come, let us build ourselves a city and a tower with its top in the heavens, and let us make a name for ourselves, lest we be dispersed over the face of the whole earth"* (Gen. 11:4). The divine directive was for mankind to divide into the nations that He had predetermined by boundaries and preappointed times in order to accomplish His will.

God's emphasis on nations within the sphere of divine purpose is somewhat foreign to the contemporary Christian worldview. We have been taught that God's purposes are centered on His personal love for us and His desire for us to experience His

---

and the development of language, the scattering of humanity into different language and culture groups was not a punishment but the intended plan from creation onward.

[48] Babel, Heb. bavel, (בבל), means confusion

"wonderful plan for our life." We are encouraged to "accept Jesus as our personal saviour." The Gospel has been individualized to the point that for the most part, as the people of God we have disassociated ourselves from the divine perspective on nations and people groups.

The Gospel reveals God's love for us as individuals. Our worth is far more than our participation in the greater whole. As Yeshua explained, *even the hairs of your head are all numbered* (Matt. 10:30). God's interest in our individuality extends to the minutest details. The Creator is aware of every facet of His creation - even the smallest bird falling to the ground does not escape His notice. In consideration of God's benevolent care for the birds, Yeshua assured us that we are *of more value than many sparrows* (Matt. 10:31).

However, the preponderance of emphasis in the scriptures is on nations and people groups. Very little of the text is directed towards individuals. This is also true of the New Testament.[49] The shift towards an individual centred Christianity is a relatively new emphasis in the Christian worldview.[50] God's purposes extend beyond His plans for us as individuals. His work is primarily centred on the consummation of all things in heaven and earth. This does not diminish our worth as individuals. When we understand that God's purposes in our life go beyond our own individual concerns, that we are part of a much bigger purpose that concerns our community and nation – even the whole world,

---

[49] Of the 27 books of the New Testament only 6 are addressed explicitly to individuals (1 Tim., 2 Tim., Titus, Philem., 2 John, 3 John [Luke and Acts are both addressed to Theophilus but were also intended for a wider audience]).

[50] Making personal decisions to "accept" Christ is a relatively new phenomenon. Altar calls originally introduced by 19th century evangelists Charles Finney and William Booth were opportunities for penitents to reflect and wait for an assurance of salvation. The move towards stepping forward to an altar as an individual decision to accept Christ as a "personal saviour" was popularized by 20th century evangelists such as Billy Sunday and later, Billy Graham. My comments are in no way intended as a criticism of any of these great men of God.

then we recognize our life has meaning beyond our own individual destiny.

God is concerned about nations because God is the author of nations. It is important that we understand that the nations are not a consequence of disobedience, or simply a human convention. The nations have a divine origin and a divine purpose. Paul goes on to explain that God's choice to create nations was so *"that they should seek God, and perhaps feel their way toward him and find him"* (Acts 17:27). God created the nations so that the nations would seek after and find God. When we consider just how much pain and suffering has been caused by nations warring against and exploiting other nations, it is hard to fathom that the nations are a good thing, and that their purpose is ultimately redemptive.

So much of God's intentions for nations have been marred by the nations' failure to submit to the will of God. The individual pull within us all towards deciding what is good and what is evil for ourselves extends to the nations as well. Instead of submitting to God, the leaders of nations have determined what is good for the nation at the expense of other nations, or even at the expense of their own citizens.

Paul's comments about the formation of nations in Acts 17 is a paraphrase of a verse from the Song of Moses:

> *"When the Most High divided their inheritance to the nations, When He separated the sons of Adam, He set the boundaries of the peoples According to the number of the children of Israel."*[51]
> (Deut. 32:8 NKJV)

The Song of Moses attributes the nations to God's intentions, noting that *"The Most High"* gave each nation an inheritance. This

---

[51] Some modern translations based on the critical text have "Sons of God" instead of "Children of Israel" but the MS Hebrew text is
"לְמִסְפַּר בְּנֵי יִשְׂרָאֵל" (Deut. 32:8), "According to the number of B'nai Yisrael" (Sons of Israel). Scriptures' emphasis on the interplay between Israel and the nations supports the MS text.

corresponds to the *"pre-appointed times"* of Acts 17:26. That the God of Israel *"set the boundaries of the peoples,"* corresponds to Paul's explanation that God set the *"boundaries of their dwellings"* (Acts 17:26). But whereas in Acts 17, Paul explains that this is so the nations might find the creator, in Deuteronomy, this is according to the number of the *"Children of Israel."*

In his speech to the Athenians in Acts 17, Paul paraphrased this Torah portion to explain that God's purpose for the nations was to seek after and find Him. The Song of Moses does not delve into God's purpose for establishing the nations, but explains that when God purposed to establish the nations, He did so with Israel in mind. According to the genealogy of nations in Genesis 10, there are 70 nations reckoned.[52] The number 70 is also the number reckoned for all of Israel's descendants,[53] equaling the number of nations reckoned in Genesis 10.

How should we understand the connection between these two passages? Surely Paul understood that the divine choice for pre-determined boundaries and the inheritance of the nations was as per Deuteronomy 32:8, *"according to the number of the children of Israel"* and yet, Acts does not directly connect God's choosing of the nations to the children of Israel. Paul's discourse to the Athenian philosophers in Acts 17 focuses rather on the outcome of God's choosing. Paul's conclusion is that God's choices for the nations were ultimately redemptive. The goal is that the nations would seek and eventually find Him.

When one considers just how much Paul's writings are focused on the connection between Israel and the nations,[54] one cannot dismiss the connection in Paul's thought between his presentation to the Athenians and Deuteronomy 32:8. Paul, the Apostle to the Gentiles was firm in his conviction that he received the Gospel by revelation while meditating alone in the desert

---

[52] The sons of Shem, Japheth and Ham totals 70. Genesis 10:32 states: "from these the nations spread abroad on the earth after the flood."
[53] Gen. 49:27; Exod. 1:5; Deut. 10:22
[54] See, Shoub. "To the Jew First" In this book the author outlines Paul's theology of Israel and the Nations as disclosed in Paul's letters to the Romans and Ephesians.

(Gal. 1:12). He explained to the Ephesians that the mystery made known to him by revelation was that the Gentiles (the Nations), were fellow heirs with Israel (Eph. 3:1-6). Paul was keenly aware of the relationship between Israel and the nations. How are we to understand Paul's reference to Deuteronomy 32:8 in light of Israel and the nations?

One of the principles of Jewish exegesis is "*Hekkesh,*" literally, hitting two stones together.[55] *Hekkesh* is a form of analogy that synthesizes the ideas contained in two verses that present different ideas but use similar words. [56] Yeshua used the interpretive principle of *Hekkesh* by combining two of the 10 commandments. Yeshua combined the ideas presented in *"You shall not commit adultery"* (Exod. 20:14), with *"You shall not covet...your neighbors wife"* (Exod. 20:17). "Hitting these two verses together" Yeshua explained that coveting your neighbor's wife is tantamount to committing adultery with her in your heart (Matt. 5:27,28).[57]

A *Hekkesh* analogy of Deuteronomy 32:8 with Acts 17:26 would conclude that the nations finding God is connected to their reckoning in relationship to the Children of Israel. In the Creator's plan for redemption and consummation, He chose one to represent the many. It was one man, Abraham, who received the redemption promise. From Abraham's progeny, Isaac was chosen and from Isaac, Jacob. Unlike his forefathers, Jacob's children were not divided between the chosen one and those not chosen. All of Jacob's 12 sons inherited the promise made to Abraham, Isaac and Jacob.

The promise made to one man expanded to one clan. Jacob's clan represented the nation of Israel in seed form. Israel is the chosen nation through whom the plan for redemption and consummation of all nations is established. The nations can only come into their destiny in relationship to the Creator's purposes and calling for Israel.

---

[55] Joseph Shulam. "Hidden Treasures" (Jerusalem, Israel: Netivyah, 2008) 65.
[56] Ibid.
[57] Ibid. 66.

We will delve into the connection between Israel and the nations when we consider the King of Israel's dual mandate over Israel and the nations in Chapter 10. The dichotomy of Israel and the nations extends throughout all of Scripture. From Genesis to Revelation the narrative of Scripture can be understood as the interplay between Israel and the nations. The first messianic promise makes no such distinction; it is the generic *"seed of the woman"* that will prevail over the Serpent. With God's choosing of Abraham, the dichotomy between Israel and the nations is established. One is chosen and blessed, but through this one all others will be blessed. The dichotomy of Israel and the nations was not intended to be oppositional or adversarial, it was intended to bring mutual benefit to both parties.

In order to accomplish this, Israel was marked off from all the other nations. When Balaam peered out over the mountains of Moab to see Israel camped on the east side of the Jordan river he declared under inspiration, *"For from the top of the crags I see him, from the hills I behold him; behold, a people dwelling alone, and not counting itself among the nations!"* (Num. 23:9). Israel was not reckoned among the nations. Jeremiah phrased it differently, referring to Israel as *"the chief of the nations"* (Jer. 31:7), but both Balaam and Jeremiah were conveying the same idea. Israel is set apart from all the other nations of the world. When we consider that the Creator reckoned all nations in relationship to the one nation not reckoned among them, we must conclude that Paul's explanation of God's intentions for the nations includes God's purposes for Israel.

God's creation mandate for humanity to rule under His ultimate authority was first redemptively focused on the *"Seed of the woman,"* one who would represent us all. With God's covenant with Abraham the focus shifted to Abraham's seed, a particular family through whom all other families would be blessed. Jacob's deathbed prophecy to his sons denoted that the king who would rule over Israel would come from Judah. Israel's king embodies the nation of Israel and represents the nation as a whole. Israel's king is also given the promise that he will rule over all the nations of the world.

CHAPTER 6

The Kings of the Earth

"Why do the nations rage and the peoples plot in vain? The kings of the earth set themselves, and the rulers take counsel together, against the LORD and against his Anointed, saying, 'Let us burst their bonds apart and cast away their cords from us.'" (Psalms 2:1–3)

I have described the fall as the first couples' decision to choose for themselves to be the final arbitrators of what is good and what is evil. They had been given a mandate to rule and were to accomplish this by multiplying and filling the earth with their progeny. The whole earth was to come under humanity's delegated authority, accomplishing the Heavenly Father's will on earth as it is in heaven. As humanity expanded to the farthest reaches of the globe, the human family would form into nations, all in keeping with God's purposes and under God's authority, all bringing honour to the Creator as they worked cooperatively to fulfill the creation mandate.

The pattern of rebellion that started with Adam and Eve continues on in us all, but in a unique way with those who have received authority to rule over nations. Psalm 2:1-3 portrays the nations in a raging rebellion against God's rule. The psalm identifies the leaders of these nations as *"the kings of the earth."*

Over the course of time Adam and Eve's decision to choose for themselves expanded into the international arena and like Adam and Eve, the international leaders refused to heed the Creator's instructions. Psalm 2 places this rebellion in the context of a unique king, chosen by God to rule over all nations.

77

Psalm 2:2 describes this king as God's anointed one, the Messiah. We will discuss the role of God's Messiah vis-a-vis the Kings of the earth in the next chapter.

The kings of the earth regard the Creator's commands as bonds to be burst apart, not as the loving counsel of the Heavenly Father who longs to see His creatures free indeed. Throughout Scripture there are multiple examples of "kings of the earth" refusing to obey Creator God. When Pharaoh is confronted by Moses to release Israel (Exod. 4.22), Pharaoh replied, *"Who is the* LORD, *that I should obey his voice and let Israel go? I do not know the* LORD, *and moreover, I will not let Israel go"* (Exod. 5:2).

Pharaoh's question was not an honest inquiry as to the identity of Israel's God. Pharaoh was regarded as a god in his own right. To say he did not know the LORD was his way of informing Moses that he did not recognize the LORD's authority over him. It would have seemed preposterous to Pharaoh to submit to a god of slaves. No one told Pharaoh what to do, certainly not a Hebrew or the Hebrews' god.

The plagues against Egypt were not just heavy handed persuaders to force Pharaoh to change his mind, they were a demonstration to Pharaoh and all Egypt that the "god" of the Hebrews was not a weak tribal deity who could not even save his tribe from bondage to the Egyptians, but the Creator who made heaven and earth and everything in it. The ten plagues demonstrated the God of Israel's sovereign power over nature, Egypt, the gods of Egypt[58] and Pharaoh. Pharaoh was powerless before Israel's God.

The Assyrian king Sennacherib displayed the same arrogance towards the God of Israel as Pharaoh had done before him:

"Then the Rabshakeh stood and called out in a loud voice in the language of Judah: "Hear the word of the great king, the king of Assyria! Thus says the king… do not listen to Hezekiah

---

[58] The 10 plagues correspond to the powers of 10 Egyptian deities. See, Chuck Missler, "The Invisible War: Against the Gods of Egypt," Koinonia House [cited July 2000]. Online: http://www.khouse.org/articles/2000/263/

when he misleads you by saying, 'The LORD *will deliver us.' Has any of the gods of the nations ever delivered his land out of the hand of the king of Assyria...Who among all the gods of the lands have delivered their lands out of my hand, that the* LORD *should deliver Jerusalem out of my hand?'"*
(2 Kings 18:28–35)

Like Pharaoh, Sennacherib regarded himself to have greater authority than the God of Israel. No other god had withstood him, therefore Israel's god would also be powerless to protect his people from Assyrian conquest. The God of Israel is the supreme authority in the universe. That a mere man would defy Him is the height of hubris:

"Whom have you mocked and reviled? Against whom have you raised your voice and lifted your eyes to the heights? Against the Holy One of Israel!" (2 Kings 19:22)

The God of Israel is not mocked. Sennacherib boasted that the God of Israel could not stop him from conquering Jerusalem. In response, the God of Israel issued the decree from heaven that it shall not be so:

"But I know your sitting down and your going out and coming in, and your raging against me. Because you have raged against me and your complacency has come into my ears, I will put my hook in your nose and my bit in your mouth, and I will turn you back on the way by which you came."
(2 Kings 19:27–28)

The God of Israel described Sennacherib's boast as *"raging."* A similar term applied to the nations in Psalm 2:1.[59] Rebellion is not simply a passive failure to obey but an active defiance, not just a failure to say yes to God but a willful no. The same pattern of

---

[59] The Hebrew words are different. In Psalm 2:1 the Hebrew is רָגַשׁ (ragash), BDB: tumult, commotion. In 2 Kings 19:27 the Hebrew is רָגַז (ragaz), BDB: Hithp. To excite oneself (to rage)

defiance was portrayed by Nebuchadnezzar, who refused to humble himself when warned in a dream that his kingdom would be taken from him until he acknowledged, *"that the Most High rules the kingdom of men and gives it to whom he will"* (Dan. 4:25).

After seven years of humiliation, the king's reason returned to him and he proclaimed to the entire kingdom:

> *"His dominion is an everlasting dominion, and his kingdom endures from generation to generation; all the inhabitants of the earth are accounted as nothing, and he does according to his will among the host of heaven and among the inhabitants of the earth; and none can stay his hand or say to him, 'What have you done?'"* (Dan. 4:34–35)

Nebuchadnezzar's grandson, Belshazzar knew that these things had taken place, but in defiance of the God of Israel he toasted the gods of Babylon with the holy vessels his grandfather plundered from the Temple in Jerusalem (Dan. 5:2-4). Unlike his grandfather who only lost the kingdom temporarily, the Persians overthrew Belshazzar's kingdom and the Babylonian empire was lost forever.

In all these examples, when confronted with the choice to submit to the God of Israel, the leaders of the known world chose defiant rebellion. They did not recognize the God of Israel's authority over the whole earth and suffered the consequences.

Psalm 2 issues a warning to world leaders:

> *"Now therefore, O kings, be wise; be warned, O rulers of the earth. Serve the LORD with fear, and rejoice with trembling. Kiss the Son, lest he be angry, and you perish in the way"* (Ps. 2:10–12)

Psalm 2 provides a way for the *"kings of the earth"* to escape judgment.[60] They are exhorted to be wise and submit to God's designated ruler. Failure to heed the warning would result in swift and severe retribution. There is a chance, however slim it may appear, that the rulers will take heed and *"kiss the Son."*[61]

If we consider that Heaven's will on earth had included national rulers from the beginning of creation, then we understand that the rebellion of kings is a matter of the rebellious heart of kings, not the office they occupied. God intended for there to be kings on the earth, but not like Pharaoh or Caesar, raised up in pride to regard themselves as gods. Rather, the "kings of the earth" were intended to serve as authorities in the nations, all in submission to the will of heaven. The Scriptures not only anticipate judgment for the kings of the earth but also redemption of the office.

"Nations will fear the name of the LORD, and all the kings of the earth will fear your glory." (Ps. 102:15)

"All the kings of the earth shall give you thanks, O LORD" (Ps. 138:4)

The Book of Revelation predicts that the kings of the earth, under the banner of the beast and the false prophet, will gather to wage war against Messiah Yeshua (Rev. 19:19,20). This confederacy of kings will refuse the warning of Psalm 2 and therefore will be utterly destroyed (Rev. 19:21). The description of the New Jerusalem that follows the final eschatological battle reveals that new "kings of the earth" will be installed to replace those who took up a rebellion against the Messiah. In Revelation 21, a new group of kings, chosen

---

[60] Isaiah 24:21 anticipates the kings of the earth facing eschatological judgment. See also Rev. 6:15; 19:19-21

[61] The term "kiss" here is a sign of submission, i.e.: "Yet I will leave seven thousand in Israel, all the knees that have not bowed to Baal, and every mouth that has not kissed him." (1 Kings 19:18)

by and submitted to God bring the glory of their kingdoms into the city to enhance its wealth and dignity:

"And the city has no need of sun or moon to shine on it, for the glory of God gives it light, and its lamp is the Lamb. By its light will the nations walk, and the kings of the earth will bring their glory into it...They will bring into it the glory and the honor of the nations." (Rev. 21:23,24,26)

At the consummation of all things there will remain kings of the earth exercising authority in the nations under the King of Kings. The establishment of Yeshua as Lord of Lords and King of kings does not remove national boundaries or national authority structures. The Kingdom of God is more than a culture or a set of principles to guide the lifestyle of the believer. It is the establishment of God's rule on earth, ultimately through the one ruler, God's Messiah. He is the king that was promised to come from David's line to rule over Israel and all peoples forever. As the victor over the Serpent, the Beast, the false prophet and the kings of the earth, he will appoint rulers to govern nations and cities on his behalf and under his authority (Luke 19:17).

The rebellion that started in the beginning by Adam and Eve, chosen to rule over the planet, will culminate with the rulers of this world waging war against God's Messiah. The solution to the rebellion of the human heart is its spiritual transformation accomplished through Yeshua's sacrificial death and triumphant resurrection. The solution to the rebellion against God's authority on planet earth is the establishment of Yeshua's reign on earth as God's designated King.

Mankind was given authority to rule the planet in submission to God's supreme authority. God's anointed, the Messiah who demonstrated his submission to God by taking the lowest place, and suffering death on a cross is the ruler raised to the highest place. All creatures in heaven and earth and below the earth will bow their knee to God's appointed ruler and declare that Yeshua is Lord of all (Phil. 2:6-11).

CHAPTER 7

God's Solution Against Rebellious Rulers

Despite the active rebellion of the kings of the earth, God has never relinquished His authority over the earth and all that is in it. As the Psalmist declared:

> *"The earth is the LORD's and the fullness thereof, the world and those who dwell therein, for he has founded it upon the seas and established it upon the rivers."* (Psalms 24:1–2)

As the Creator, God by right has ownership and therefore complete authority over the planet. As I noted in my introduction, paintings do not instruct artists nor do musical scores resist composers. Pots never question the potter asking *"why have you made me like this?"* (Rom. 9:20). Creatures, no matter how wonderfully gifted with godlike faculties are in no more solid a position to question the Creator anymore than artistic works can question their creators. By definition, any creator has authority over the creation he or she has made. When the ruling authorities in Jerusalem threatened the apostles, commanding them not to preach in the name of Yeshua, the apostles appealed to God's higher authority as the Creator of the world:

> *"When they were released, they went to their friends and reported what the chief priests and the elders had said to them. And when they heard it, they lifted their voices together to God and said, 'Sovereign Lord, who made the heaven and the earth and the sea and everything in them "who through the mouth of our father David, your servant, said by the Holy Spirit, 'Why did the Gentiles rage, and the peoples plot in vain? The kings of the earth set themselves, and the rulers were gathered together, against the Lord and against his Anointed... Lord,*

look upon their threats and grant to your servants to continue to speak your word with all boldness, while you stretch out your hand to heal, and signs and wonders are performed through the name of your holy servant Jesus."
(Acts 4:23-26, 29–30)

Following their appeal to God as the Creator, the apostles quoted from Psalm 2:1-3. As we have already explored, the psalm portrays the *"kings of the earth"* in rebellion against the Creator. The council in Jerusalem had displayed the same kind of rebellion expressed in Psalm 2. They resisted God's will by arresting the apostles and forbidding them from preaching in the name of Yeshua. The apostles asked God to take note of their threats and increase their boldness and anointing, so as to preach in the name of Yeshua with even greater effectiveness.

In Psalm 2, God's answer to the rebellion of worldly rulers was to establish His own ruler who would carry out His will on the earth:

"He who sits in the heavens laughs; the Lord holds them in derision. Then he will speak to them in his wrath, and terrify them in his fury, saying, 'As for me, I have set my King on Zion, my holy hill.'" (Psalms 2:4–6)

The answer to the rebellion of kings is the establishment of another king, God's king ruling at heaven's direction, from God's holy hill of Zion. The rebellion has no chance of success – it is so absurd as to make God laugh in derision at those creatures, who so deceived by their own hubris, assume that they can put off any constraint imposed by heaven's will. But their rebellion will not be nullified by fire from heaven. Instead, their power is threatened by an alternative earthly power that will obey God's commands and is therefore endued with God's authority to rule on planet earth. God has a chosen king who will represent him as a son represents his father.

Psalm 2 informs us that God's king is God's son:

"I will tell of the decree: The L*ORD said to me, "You are my Son; today I have begotten you."* (Psalms 2:7)

Psalm 2:7 refers back to the decree that established God's king as God's son. For most Christians, the term "son of God" refers to Yeshua's divine status as the son from heaven – even "God the Son"[62] as He is described in the Trinitarian formula. Not withstanding the Christological nuances of the term "Son of God," originally, it was not used to convey divine status but was a title for Israel's king.[63] The decree was God's promise to David of an enduring dynasty and that the ruler who would come from his line would be God's son:[64]

"When your days are fulfilled and you lie down with your fathers, I will raise up your offspring after you, who shall come from your body, and I will establish his kingdom. He shall build a house for my name, and I will establish the throne of his kingdom forever. I will be to him a father, and he shall be to me a son." (2 Sam. 7:12–14)

---

[62] The term "God the Son" is not found within Scripture. However, referring to Yeshua's deity, Paul employs the filial term, "firstborn of all creation" (Col. 1:15).

[63] Boyarin, "The Jewish Gospels" 28.

[64] 2 Samuel 7 promised David that "your house and your kingdom shall be made sure forever before me. Your throne shall be established forever." (2 Sam. 7:16) The passage includes a proviso that should any of David's heirs commit iniquity they would be punished. In 1 Chronicles 17 (the parallel version of God's promise to David), there is no reference to the potential punishment of David's heir (s). Whereas the 2 Samuel passage emphasizes David's throne being established despite the potential disobedience of his heirs, the Chronicles version, much like Psalm 2 emphasizes the unique reign of one of David's heirs, "and his throne shall be established forever." (1 Chron. 17: 14)

The declaration that the king of Israel is God's son is a re-focusing of the declaration that Israel is God's son. Prior to Moses appearing before Pharaoh to demand he release Israel from bondage, God instructed Moses to explain to Pharaoh, *"Thus says the LORD, Israel is my firstborn son"* (Exod. 4:22). Sonship indicates a relationship of chosenness and representation. God's declaration that Israel is His son set Israel apart from other nations as the Creator's representative nation, and placed Israel within a relationship of love and intimacy with Father God. In 2 Samuel 7, this unique chosenness is re-emphasized to Israel's king, thereby establishing the king as God's personal representative to the nation. As we will see, this is very significant.

As the supreme authority, God grants His king in Zion rulership over all nations.

> *"Ask of me, and I will make the nations your heritage, and the ends of the earth your possession."* (Psalms 2:8)

Psalm 2:8 has been utilized in missionary endeavors as God's promise to grant evangelistic success in foreign countries. Missionaries have been encouraged to ask God for specific countries based on the promise of this verse. I am sure God is interested in the success of missionary activity, but this is not the meaning of God's promise respecting the inheritance of the nations. The promise is made to God's son. The nations are his inheritance, and the ends of the earth his possession.

The kings of the earth, set in rebellion against God and His appointed king have the foundation of their power removed by God's promise to give all the nations to His king for an inheritance. Unlike the kings of the earth, God's king does God's will and therefore is granted authority to rule over all nations. God can do this, because as He declared when He chose Israel above all others, *"All the earth is mine"* (Exod. 19:5). The promise made to all of humanity through the first couple in Genesis 1:28 is now collapsed into an authority bestowed on a single individual, God's chosen king. He is designated as God's appointed ruler to have dominion over the birds of the air, the fish of the sea and everything that moves upon the face of the earth. God's appointed king has his throne on God's holy hill of Zion (Ps. 2:6). God's appointed king rules from Jerusalem – He is Israel's king.

Usually, when we consider Yeshua as God's king we picture his divine splendor and authority. He is Lord of Lords and King of Kings, having received all authority in heaven and earth and now seated far above all principalities and powers.

This is a true picture of the risen Yeshua but in one sense it is incomplete. With respect to Yeshua's status as a human being, he has received his authority over the nations because he is God's appointed king, the heir promised to David whose rule would never end. It is the king of Israel who is promised all nations as his inheritance. In this sense, he is the King of Kings because he is the king of Israel – he is not the king of Israel because he is the King of Kings. Because Yeshua, David's heir and God's appointed king represents His Heavenly Father, the Father, creator of all, owner of the planet and everything in it, grants the nations of the world to His son as the son's inheritance (Ps. 2:8).

The promise originally made to David is that his line would endure forever as kings over Israel. The 1 Chronicles version of this promise foretells a specific heir who will reign over Israel forever. The promise is expanded in Psalm 2 to extend beyond reigning over Israel to reigning over the whole world. As Psalm 72 declares, the borders of the realm of God's appointed king move beyond the boundaries of Israel to include the whole earth, *"He shall have dominion also from sea to sea, And from the River to the ends of the earth"* (Ps. 72:8 NKJV).

This promise of Israel's king as ruler over the world is in keeping with Daniel's vision of God's appointed ruler:

> *"I saw in the night visions, and behold, with the clouds of heaven there came one like a son of man, and he came to the Ancient of Days and was presented before him. And to him was given dominion and glory and a kingdom, that all peoples, nations, and languages should serve him; his dominion*

is an everlasting dominion, which shall not pass away, and his kingdom one that shall not be destroyed." (Dan. 7:13–14)

In Daniel's vision it is not God's son who receives an eternal kingdom, nor is Israel primarily in view. *"One like a son of man"* receives an everlasting kingdom over *"all peoples, nations, and languages."*

The "son of God" and the "son of man"[65] are both titles for Yeshua. Yeshua is the king of Israel anticipated by Psalm 2 and the "son of man" who Daniel saw in his vision of heaven's throne room. He has been granted authority over all nations and peoples. According to Psalm 72:8, his dominion extends beyond Israel's western boundary at the Mediterranean Sea, its eastern boundary at the Dead Sea and its northern border at the Euphrates River. The boundaries of Yeshua's kingdom encompass the ends of the earth. This echoes the declaration in Psalm 2:8, that the nations are his inheritance and the ends of the earth his possession.

This radically shifts our focus with respect to Israel and the kingdom of God. Israel is not just the vehicle to bring God's ruler into the world. It is the chosen nation through which God's ruler activates his authority over the whole planet. The promise is made to David that his throne would endure forever through a descendent whose reign would never end.

This promise has covenant status conferring onto it the assurance of covenant fidelity:

---

[65] The Hebrew term "son of man", ben adam (בֶּן־אָדָם), can simply mean human being (Ezek. 2:1ff). In Daniel 7 the term is Aramaic, bar enash (בַּר אֱנָשׁ), but corresponds to the Hebrew ben adam. In the Daniel passage the son of man is a heavenly being with divine authority. Daniel sees two thrones in heaven's court (Dan. 7:9). One for the Ancient of Days and one for the Son of Man who receives dominion to rule over the planet. In this sense, Son of Man is not equivalent to human being, but a title for God's ruler. This adds significance to Yeshua's self identification as the Son of Man. This was not a sign of humility but a declaration that he is God's appointed ruler (i.e. Matt. 12:8; Mark 2:10; 14:61,62). See, Boyarin. "The Jewish Gospels" 35-40.

"I have made a covenant with my chosen one; I have sworn to David my servant: 'I will establish your offspring forever, and build your throne for all generations." (Ps. 89:3–4)

Because the promise has covenant status, it moves the promise beyond a personal boon to David and his children into the broader purposes and plans of God. The seed of the woman who would crush the serpent's head, who would restore authority on the planet to humanity under God's will and sovereignty, is God's chosen king, David's heir, the king of Israel. To this one is given divine authority to rule and have dominion over all peoples and all places (Ps. 2:8; Dan. 7:13,14).

Currently Yeshua is seated at the right hand of his father in heaven but the day will come when he returns to sit on his throne in Jerusalem. Ultimately, Jerusalem will be transformed, coming down out of heaven to earth. But the New Jerusalem is still Jerusalem. This is why Yeshua instructed his disciples not to swear by Jerusalem, *"for it is the city of the great king"* (Matt. 5:35).

Many Christians who sympathize with Israel make much of the command to *"pray for the peace of Jerusalem"*[66] (Ps. 122:6). This is a worthy endeavor but it seems that too often the command is separated from the grounds from which the imperative emerges. The Psalmist explained that one is to pray for the city's peace because, *"there thrones for judgment were set, the thrones of the house of David"* (Ps. 122:5).

Because Jerusalem is the city God has chosen for the throne of His appointed ruler, all should seek its welfare. I am an Israeli citizen and certainly very sympathetic to Jerusalem's welfare, but this text goes beyond political or cultural considerations, at least in the regular sense of politics and culture. Psalm 122:6 is focused

---

[66] The Hebrew reads, שַׁאֲלוּ שְׁלוֹם יְרוּשָׁלָ͏ִם shalu shalom yerushalem, "ask or inquire [of YHVH] for Jerusalem's peace." Though the typical Hebrew word for prayer is not used, the sense is inquiring of the LORD on Jerusalem's behalf. TWOT, Harris; Archer, Jr., Waltke, Copyright © 1980 by The Moody Bible Institute of Chicago Electronic text used by permission. P. 981

on the expectation of God's *"Shalom"* emanating across the globe from the *"City of the Great King."* Praying for the peace of Jerusalem is not foremost an intercession for violence to end in the city. The Hebrew word for peace, *shalom* "means much more than mere absence of war." More to the point, Shalom indicates wholeness, completeness and fulfillment."[67]

Asking God to bring peace to Jerusalem is recognition that God's shalom will be restored to planet earth by God's appointed ruler in Jerusalem. The Son of Man/Son of God has been granted authority to rule on God's behalf over Israel and the nations. To pray for the peace of Jerusalem is essentially another way to pray, *"Your kingdom come, Your will be done on earth as it is in heaven."*

As discussed in the previous chapter, the last section of Psalm 2 is a warning to the Kings of the earth:

> *"Now therefore, O kings, be wise; be warned, O rulers of the earth. Serve the LORD with fear, and rejoice with trembling. Kiss the Son, lest he be angry, and you perish in the way, for his wrath is quickly kindled. Blessed are all who take refuge in him."* (Ps. 2:9–12)

The warning includes the hope of redemption. The rulers have a choice: submit to God's appointed king or *"perish in the way."* The final word of Psalm 2 is not judgment but blessing. All who submit to God's king, those who recognize his authority are not bound in chains and chords that restrict, rather they find a refuge of safety and shalom and are blessed. God's king will execute God's judgment. The world order must be returned to proper submission to God's authority but the Messiah's mission has always been restorative - He first came and will return to restore blessing to the planet and to humanity.

---

[67] TWOT, Harris; Archer, Jr., Waltke,
Copyright © 1980 by The Moody Bible Institute of Chicago
Electronic text used by permission. Vol. 2 p.931

CHAPTER 8

Yeshua is Israel's King

The Hebrew Scriptures portray the Messiah as God's anointed king. The New Testament Scriptures also portray Messiah as God's anointed king. However, within all the gospels, and especially within the Synoptic gospels there is a certain downplaying of Yeshua's messianic kingship. He healed people and instructed them to keep the matter a secret (Mark 5:41).[68] He addressed the crowds with parables that were purposely ambiguous (Matt. 13:10-15). When rulers confronted Yeshua about his authority, he avoided a direct answer to the question by answering with another question (Luke 20:1-3). When the crowd sought to make him king, he ran away (John 6:15). Throughout the telling of Yeshua's story as Messiah there runs a theme demonstrating that the Messiah revealed to Israel was not the Messiah Israel expected.

Perhaps the best example is Luke' account of the two disciples on the road to Emmaus:

> *"That very day two of them were going to a village named Emmaus...While they were talking and discussing together, Jesus himself drew near and went with them...And he said to them, "What is this conversation that you are holding with each other as you walk?" And they stood still, looking sad. Then one of them, named Cleopas, answered him, "Are you the only visitor to Jerusalem who does not know the things that have happened there in these days?" And he said to them,*

---

[68] Mark's gospel records the most occasions wherein Yeshua instructed witnesses not to tell anyone what they saw (Mark 5:41; 7:34; 8:28; 9:9).

"What things?" And they said to him, "Concerning Jesus of Nazareth, a man who was a prophet mighty in deed and word before God and all the people, and how our chief priests and rulers delivered him up to be condemned to death, and crucified him. But we had hoped that he was the one to redeem Israel." (Luke 24:13–21)

Like all of Israel, these two disciples were expecting the king Messiah who would *"redeem Israel."* Yeshua's ministry had demonstrated the necessary Messianic signs. His birth was miraculous and accompanied by signs and wonders. He performed miracles like Elijah and Elisha but to a far greater measure. He bestowed Torah (that is, instruction)[69] that in some cases superseded Moses; a *Bat Kol* (A voice from Heaven) declared him to be the Son of God, even the winds on the sea obeyed him.[70]

Yeshua himself declared he was the Messiah but only to a select few, usually under special circumstances. He knew who he was, but he downplayed his kingly office because he knew the vital importance of the priestly dimension of his messiahship:

"And he said to them, 'O foolish ones, and slow of heart to believe all that the prophets have spoken! Was it not necessary that the Christ should suffer these things and enter into his glory?'" (Luke 24:25–26)

We will explore the ramifications of Yeshua's priestly ministry in chapter 9. However, as vital as Yeshua's priestly ministry is, to some extent the emphasis among believers on Yeshua's priestly ministry has overshadowed Yeshua's identity as king. It is true that all four gospels' emphasize Yeshua's priestly ministry. For the most part, the gospel narratives are the story of how the Messiah suffered so that he could *"enter into his glory."* However, a careful reading of the gospels demonstrates that all four gospel writers

---

[69] The sense of the Hebrew word Torah is instruction more so than law.
[70] Compare Matt. 8:27 and Psalm 107:28,29

were very concerned with Yeshua's identity as king. There is a trend within our understanding of Christology, cued by the gospel writers' correction of Israel's messianic expectations that emphasizes Yeshua's priestly identity over his kingly identity. More so, on a practical level Christians have related to Yeshua more as saviour than as king. This is understandable because all of us have entered into God's kingdom through Yeshua's priestly ministry.

There are exceedingly good reasons why we cherish and worship Yeshua as our saviour. In heaven, *"the Lamb that was slain"* receives continual angelic praise and adoration (Rev. 5:12-14). All that he suffered not only ushered him into his glorious exaltation, it redeemed all of us from bondage to sin and death. One can never underestimate the value of Yeshua's priestly salvation. As believers we cannot begin to relate to all that Yeshua is to us, without first embracing his salvation for us as individuals. Even with respect to his kingdom, we only gain access as citizens of his kingdom through his saving efficacy. Without downplaying Yeshua identity as saviour, it is my intention to help re-focus our attention on Yeshua's identity as king.

One cannot truly divide between Yeshua's priesthood and his kingship. Describing Yeshua as a priest and also as a king is in a sense an artificial construct. Yeshua is at the same time, both a priest who rules and a king who serves.[71] Yeshua's rule/priesthood reflect the divine character of a love that serves and an authority that rules. They are indivisible because they reflect the nature of the Godhead. For the sake of clarity on how these two elements of Yeshua's identity are connected and function, I am in a sense purposely making a distinction between Yeshua's priestly ministry and kingly rule.

I would contend that even for the gospel writers, Yeshua's kingly identity is their foremost emphasis – or at least emphasized by them to the same extent as Yeshua's priestly role. Matthew began his gospel with Yeshua's genealogy, identifying Yeshua as

---

[71] My thanks to Dr. Mark Kinzer for this helpful instruction, from an email correspondence received July 1, 2018

"the son of David, the son of Abraham" (Matt. 1:1). Matthew informed his readers that Yeshua is the heir to the covenant promises made to Abraham and David. Ultimately, it is through Yeshua that all the families of the earth receive blessings. Yeshua is David's heir, the king whose rule over Israel and the nations endures forever.

Matthew emphasized Yeshua's genealogy through the kingly line extended down from David through Solomon, and the kings of Judah that followed within the Davidic dynasty.[72] The fact that Matthew placed Yeshua's Davidic credentials at the start of his gospel indicates its importance in Matthew's gospel. Matthew intended his readers to understand that Yeshua was the long awaited heir to David's kingdom from the line of David's royal house.

Mark does not include a genealogy. The first line of Mark's gospel is, *"The beginning of the gospel of Jesus Christ, the Son of God"* (Mark 1:1). As discussed above, *"Son of God"* has strong Davidic undertones. In Mark's gospel, the first words of Yeshua are, *"The time is fulfilled, and the kingdom of God is at hand; repent and believe in the gospel"* (Mark 1:15). The term "gospel" is loaded with theological meaning centered around Yeshua's priestly service. It has become a singularly "Christian" term. However, Yeshua began his ministry preaching the "gospel" to Jews living in Galilee. For these Galileans the term gospel already had significant meaning, even if they could not grasp the measure to which Yeshua's priestly sacrifice made this "good news" good.

---

[72] Luke recorded Yeshua's genealogy beyond Abraham to Adam. In Luke's gospel Yeshua's ancestry passes through David to David's son Nathan. Harmonization of Matthew and Luke's genealogies is difficult. The standard explanation for the differentiation is that Matthew's genealogy covers Yeshua' legal claim to the throne as Joseph's legal son and Luke's genealogy covers Yeshua's physical claim to the throne as a blood relative of David through his mother, Miriam (Mary).

The term gospel, or good news[73] is first used in the Hebrew Scriptures for the message dispatched from the battlefield by a courier, announcing victory over enemy combatants. Watchmen on the walls of the city would be on the lookout for a runner bringing the news. When Joab and David's men defeated Absalom's conspiracy, Joab sent a runner to announce the news[74] of victory back to David. Later Isaiah used the same term to speak of the God of Israel's ultimate victory over Israel's enemies.[75]

"How beautiful upon the mountains are the feet of him who brings good news, who publishes peace, who brings good news of happiness, who publishes salvation, who says to Zion, 'Your God reigns.' The voice of your watchmen—they lift up their voice; together they sing for joy; for eye to eye they see the return of the LORD to Zion. Break forth together into singing, you waste places of Jerusalem, for the LORD has comforted his people; he has redeemed Jerusalem. The LORD has bared his holy arm before the eyes of all the nations, and all the ends of the earth shall see the salvation of our God." (Isa. 52:7–10)

In Isaiah's vision of the heralding of the good news, the courier announcing the victory is none other than the LORD Himself, returning to Zion, baring His holy arm in salvation and restoration. Isaiah's "gospel" is not simply "Jesus died for our sins," but the expectation of Israel's ultimate deliverance and restoration. It is the establishment of God's kingdom on earth. Therefore, when Yeshua called the Jews of Galilee to *"believe the gospel,"* he was announcing God's victory, that is, *"the kingdom of God is at hand."* The gospel, the good news is the good news about God's kingdom. The gospel is not only the story of Yeshua's priestly ministry; rather it is the story of how through Yeshua's priestly

---

[73] Gospel is the English equivalent of the Greek word εὐαγγέλιον (yoo-ang-ghel´-ee-on). This is the root of the English terms evangelize and evangelical.

[74] *The Hebrew term for good news is* בשׂר (basar), to bear (good) tidings. *BDB*

[75] TWOT, Vol. 1. P. 136

ministry he *"enter[ed] into his glory"* as God's appointed king, the Messiah.

We also see this primary emphasis on Yeshua as king in the beginning of Luke and John's gospels. In Luke chapter 1, Gabriel's message to Miriam (Mary) emphasized Yeshua's kingly identity:

> *"And behold, you will conceive in your womb and bear a son, and you shall call his name Jesus. He will be great and will be called the Son of the Most High. And the Lord God will give to him the throne of his father David, and he will reign over the house of Jacob forever, and of his kingdom there will be no end.'"* (Luke 1:31–33)

Gabriel's announcement combined prophetic elements of Psalm 2:6, that Yeshua will be called *"the Son of God,"* 2 Samuel 7:16, that Yeshua *"will reign over the house of Jacob forever,"* and Daniel 7:14, *"and of his kingdom there will be no end."* All these elements emphasize Yeshua as king. That Yeshua reigns over the house of Jacob forever has tremendous significance. We will address Yeshua's eternal fidelity to Israel below.

John's gospel directly links Yeshua as Son of God to Yeshua as king of Israel: *"Nathanael said to him, 'How do you know me?' Jesus answered him, 'Before Philip called you, when you were under the fig tree, I saw you.' Nathanael answered him, 'Rabbi, you are the Son of God! You are the King of Israel'"* (John 1:48–49). All four gospels begin their narratives with passages emphasizing Yeshua's identity as the Son of David/Son of God, king of Israel.

The central drama of the gospels is Yeshua's crucifixion and subsequent resurrection. This is the heart of Yeshua's priestly ministry. Yeshua interceded on behalf of all sinful humanity, as the Writer of Hebrews wrote, *"not by means of the blood of goats and calves but by means of his own blood, thus securing an eternal redemption"* (Heb. 9:12). However, in all four gospels' description of this great priestly act, the writers include a description of Rome's indictment against Yeshua. A sign was posted on his cross explaining that he was condemned to death for being *"King of the Jews."*[76]

The one born to *"reign over the house of Jacob forever"* was crucified for being Israel's king. The hallmark of the king of Israel was to be his absolute fidelity and obedience to God's commands. The obedience of Yeshua, king of the Jews was marked by his willingness to submit to death on the cross as a priest for all mankind. His declaration, *"Father... not my will, but yours, be done"* (Luke 22:42), was the ultimate declaration that he feared the LORD his God, kept the words of Torah and did them (Deut. 17:19). Yeshua's obedience to endure the cross demonstrated his sole legitimacy as God's appointed king.

Yeshua's own testimony in the gospels emphasized his identity as king. All three synoptics record Yeshua's trial before the Sanhedrin. Yeshua's trial was stymied by the lack of corroboration between witnesses. Exasperated by their failure to convict Yeshua of a crime, Caiaphas demanded Yeshua testify, putting him under oath, *"I adjure you by the living God, tell us if you are the Christ, the Son of God "* (Matt. 26:63). The significance of Caiaphas' question sometimes gets lost in our theological familiarity with the term "Son of God" as a reference to Yeshua's divinity. Taken in its Jewish context, the High Priest was asking Yeshua if he was the Messiah, Israel's king. Yeshua answered in the affirmative, *"But I tell you, from now on you will see the Son of Man seated at the right hand of Power and coming on the clouds of heaven"* (Matt. 26:64)[77].

Yeshua's answer is a conflation of two scriptures together, the affirmation of Israel's messianic king seated at the LORD's right hand (Ps. 110:1), and Daniel's heavenly vision of a divine ruler receiving kingship from the Ancient of Days over all the peoples of earth (Dan. 7:14). The message could not be clearer; Yeshua is

---

[76] Matt. 27:37; Mark 15:26; Luke 23:38; John 19:19. Because Yeshua is the king who suffers, the indictment, "King of the Jews" was attached to his cross. Thanks to Dr. Kinzer for this insight, from an email correspondence, July 1, 2018. (see, pg. 95)

[77] Mark's version is almost identical, Luke does not include the reference to Daniel 7:14

God's appointed ruler over Israel and *"all peoples, nations and languages."*

John's gospel does not record this dialogue between Yeshua and Caiaphas. Instead John includes a unique exchange between Yeshua and Pilate. The questioning is in a very similar vein. Pilate asked, *"So you are a king?"* To which Yeshua replied, *"You say that I am a king. For this purpose I was born"* (John 18:37).

When we consider that each gospel writer emphasized Yeshua's kingship at the beginning of their narrative, that they all testified that Yeshua was crucified for being Israel's king, and all include Yeshua's own testimony to Jewish and Gentile leaders that he is king, we have a compelling testimony from the gospel writers of Yeshua's core identity as king.

In fact, on balance all of the New Testament has a significant, if not central focus on Yeshua's identity as king. By far the most referenced Old Testament scripture within the corpus of the New Testament is Psalm 110:1, *"The LORD says to my Lord: 'Sit at my right hand, until I make your enemies your footstool'"* (Ps. 110:1).[78] Emphasis and repetition is a rhetorical device to stress importance. It is not Isaiah 53, or Psalm 22, or even Psalm 16's declaration of Messiahs resurrection that the New Testament writers emphasized, but the Messianic psalm that declares Messiah's regal victory over all enemies as God's appointed king.

The Scriptures testify that Messiah had to suffer to enter into his glory. Therefore that suffering is holy, holy, holy. It is in some ways beyond human comprehension to understand how holy God incarnate could suffer and die and behalf of sinful humanity. We will worship the Lamb of God for eternity as the one who saved us by his own blood. He is worthy to open the scroll of God's final consummation purposes because in his complete submission to his Heavenly Father, he was *"slain, and by [his] blood [he] ransomed people for God from every tribe and language and people and nation"* (Rev. 5:9).

---

[78] Ps 110:1 is referenced 22 times, far more than any other Old Testament scripture

It is the Lion of the Tribe of Judah, the king of Israel who has prevailed through suffering and humility to enter into his glory. Because of his obedience to suffer death on the cross, serving as God's great high priest, he was confirmed as God's appointed king to rule over all nations and re-establish God's rule over the planet.

CHAPTER 9

The King is a Priest

"The LORD *says to my Lord: 'Sit at my right hand, until I make your enemies your footstool.' The* LORD *sends forth from Zion your mighty scepter. Rule in the midst of your enemies! Your people will offer themselves freely on the day of your power, in holy garments; from the womb of the morning, the dew of your youth will be yours. The* LORD *has sworn and will not change his mind, 'You are a priest forever after the order of Melchizedek.'"* (Ps. 110:1–4)

Yeshua is God's appointed ruler in Zion, the King of Israel. Most messianic passages in the Hebrew Scriptures are focused on Messiah's rule over Israel and all the earth. The primary characteristics of his rule are to be peace and justice across the whole world. As Isaiah proclaimed:

"Of the increase of his government and of peace there will be no end, on the throne of David and over his kingdom, to establish it and to uphold it with justice and with righteousness from this time forth and forevermore." (Isa. 9:7)

"For the earth shall be full of the knowledge of the LORD *as the waters cover the sea."* (Isa. 11:9)

The disciples were dismayed when the Roman authorities arrested Yeshua, and crucified him as just another one of the many thousands of Jews executed by Rome. The disciples walking on the road to Emmaus lamented, *"we had hoped that he was the one to redeem Israel"* (Luke 24:21).

The greatest Jewish objection to Yeshua's messiahship is not so much a rejection of his divine status, but his seeming failure to usher in the messianic kingdom. The objection is that if Yeshua were the Messiah, then he would have *"redeemed Israel."* Current conditions on planet earth are not justice and righteousness without end, nor is the earth full of the knowledge of the Lord.[79] This is a reasonable concern regarding Yeshua's messianic credentials, because the preponderance of the Hebrew Scripture's messianic promises relate to messiah's rule over Israel and the planet.

Therefore it is not surprising that the writer of the letter to the Hebrews addressed this issue.

> *"You have crowned him with glory and honor, putting everything in subjection under his feet.' Now in putting everything in subjection to him, he left nothing outside his control. At present, we do not yet see everything in subjection to him. But we see him who for a little while was made lower than the angels, namely Jesus, crowned with glory and honor because of the suffering of death, so that by the grace of God he might taste death for everyone."* (Heb. 2:7–9)

The circumstances, authorship, and purposes of the Book of Hebrews are the subjects of ongoing debate within theological literature. There are a number of pastoral and theological purposes for the letter, but the content is mostly centred on Yeshua as High Priest after the order of Melchizedek. It is my

---

[79] This was one of the primary arguments presented by Rabbi Nachmanides during the Barcelona Disputations, 1263 ACE. R. Nachmanides purportedly stated, "from the time of Jesus until the present the world has been filled with violence and injustice, and the Christians have shed more blood than all other peoples."
Haim Beinart, "BARCELONA, DISPUTATION OF" Encyclopedia Judaica [cited 10 June 2018].
Online: https://www.jewishvirtuallibrary.org/disputation-of-barcelona

opinion that this is primarily to answer the question arising out of Hebrews 2:8, "If Yeshua is the Messiah, why do we not yet see everything in subjection to him?" The short answer is, *that by the grace of God he might taste death for everyone.*"

Psalm 110 declared that the messianic ruler is also an eternal priest after the order of Melchizedek (Ps. 110:4). Within the Mosaic covenant there is a clear distinction between priest and king.[80] King Uzziah was struck with leprosy when he presumed to take on priestly duties, by offering incense within the temple (2 Chron. 26:16-18). According to the Mosaic covenant, only descendants of Aaron could be priests. During the first temple period, neither in the southern kingdom of Judah, nor in the northern kingdom of Israel did any son of Aaron serve as king.[81] In Judah, only those in David's line served as kings. However, along with Psalm 110, the Book of Zechariah also speaks of Messiah as both king and priest:

"Behold, the man whose name is the Branch: for he shall branch out from his place, and he shall build the temple of the LORD. It is he who shall build the temple of the LORD and shall bear royal honor, and shall sit and rule on his throne. And there shall be a priest on his throne" (Zech. 6:12–13)

The Zechariah passage is in one sense speaking about the High Priest in the days of Zerubbabel, Joshua[82] the son of Jehozadak (Zech. 6:10). However, the passage also refers to the king/priest as a *"man whose name is the Branch"*(Zech. 6:12). This is an echo of Jeremiah's designation for the Messiah:

---

[80] In practice, this distinction was not always so clear – especially during David's reign, *i.e.* 1 Chron. 21:26.

[81] Later in the Hasmonean period (140-37 BCE), most of Israel/Judah was ruled by kings who were descendants of Aaron.

[82] It is not lost on the author that the name of the High Priest is Joshua (יְהוֹשֻׁעַ). This is the formal version of the name Yeshua (ישוע).

"Behold, the days are coming, declares the LORD, when I will raise up for David a righteous Branch,[83] and he shall reign as king and deal wisely, and shall execute justice and righteousness in the land." (Jer. 23:5)

Further, Psalm 110 proclaims that the king is a priest forever. This also echoes the promise made to David that the Messiah who would come from his seed would rule over Israel forever (1 Chron. 17:14).[84]

The writer of Hebrews understood the eternal designation of the Melchizedek priesthood to be connected to the Melchizedek of Genesis 14. Melchizedek,[85] the king of Salem[86] was described as *"priest of God Most High"* (Gen. 14:18). Later in Joshua 10:1, we read of Adonizedek, king of Jerusalem. It seems likely that Adonizedek and Melchizedek are variants of the same name,[87] and therefore functioned as a title much like Pharaoh in Egypt and Abimelech in Philistia. Because Melchizedek, the king of Salem was also a priest, one can conclude that the ruler of Jerusalem was also the priest for the city, therefore when David conquered Jerusalem he would have received this title as well.[88]

The writer of Hebrews makes a midrash of Psalm 110:4 to explain that the one to rule at God's right hand is a priest – not a honorary title as was conferred on David as conqueror of Jerusalem, but a functioning, eternal priest outside the regulations and limitations of the Mosaic covenant's Levitical priesthood. The writer of Hebrews answers the question as to why we do not

---

[83] Most English translations also include the messianic title, "Branch" in Isaiah (Isa. 11:1). The Hebrew word in Isaiah is *netzer (נצר)*, the word in Isa. 4:2; Jer. 23:5, 33:15 and Zech. 6:12 is Tzemakh (צמח). However, the Isaiah 11 passage is clearly referring to Messiah, see, page 110 below.

[84] See pages 51,52 above.

[85] Literally, king of righteousness

[86] Hebrew, *shalem* (שלם), that is, Jerusalem

[87] *Adonizedek*: my lord is righteous, *Melchizedek*: my king is righteous. Alec Moyter. "Look to the Rock" (IVP: Leicester, UK, 1996) 36.

[88] Ibid. This would be akin to the Pope receiving the ancient Roman priestly title of Pontus Maximus.

see all things in subjection to Messiah Yeshua by explaining that the Messiah king is also a priest. Not a priest subject to the constraints of the Levitical priesthood, but a priest who lives forever after the order of Melchizedek. Melchizedek prefigured Messiah Yeshua because he too was king of Jerusalem and priest of God Most High.

The writer of Hebrews extrapolates on Melchizedek's lack of genealogy to infer that *"without father or mother or genealogy, having neither beginning of days nor end of life, but resembling the Son of God he continues a priest forever"* (Heb. 7:3). Melchizedek "resembles" the Son of God. Yeshua's sacrificial death was the ultimate priestly service, his resurrection and ascension the validation of his eternal priestly office.

Unlike Levitical priests who had to offer yearly sacrifices for their own sins and the sins of the people (Heb. 10:1), Yeshua offered one sacrifice, once and for all time that had eternal benefit on behalf of the recipients of that sacrifice (Heb. 7:23-25). Unlike the Levitical priests, he did not offer the blood of substitutionary animals within a sanctuary, which was an earthly copy of heavenly realities, but he presented the sacrifice of his own blood within the true temple in heaven.

"For Christ has entered, not into holy places made with hands, which are copies of the true things, but into heaven itself, now to appear in the presence of God on our behalf. Nor was it to offer himself repeatedly, as the high priest enters the holy places every year with blood not his own, for then he would have had to suffer repeatedly since the foundation of the world. But as it is, he has appeared once for all at the end of the ages to put away sin by the sacrifice of himself. And just as it is appointed for man to die once, and after that comes judgment, so Christ, having been offered once to bear the sins of many, will appear a second time, not to deal with sin but to save those who are eagerly waiting for him." (Heb. 9:24–28)

Yeshua is the king/priest. In him, the picture first presented in Zechariah of a priest ruling on his throne (Zech. 6:12,13) is fully realized. The critical issue is that like all priesthoods, Yeshua's priesthood was not for his benefit but completely for the sake of others. As the writer of Hebrews explained, Yeshua *"taste[d] death for everyone,"* so that he could *"bring many sons to glory"* (Heb. 2:9,10).

> *"Since therefore the children share in flesh and blood, he himself likewise partook of the same things, that through death he might destroy the one who has the power of death, that is, the devil, and deliver all those who through fear of death were subject to lifelong slavery."* (Heb. 2:14–15)

Yeshua's priestly sacrifice was to deliver *"the children"* from the power of death. As children rescued from death we are profoundly grateful for Yeshua's sacrifice. We remember the New Covenant, cut in his blood, by partaking of the bread and wine, his body broken and his blood shed for us. To reiterate what I have already said above, Yeshua's saving sacrificial death can never be understated. Yeshua bears the marks of his crucifixion for eternity, and for eternity is worshipped as *"The Lamb that was slain."*

However, in so far as Yeshua's death was the greatest act of love and redemption ever made, the salvation it accomplished was not an end in itself. Yeshua's priestly role is unto the re-establishment of God's rule and order on planet earth. As High Priest after the order of Melchizedek, Yeshua offered the required sacrifice to nullify death, and cancel the power of death over humanity and all creation. As Paul explained:

> *"Sin came into the world through one man, and death through sin, and so death spread to all men because all sinned…But the free gift is not like the trespass… For if, because of one man's trespass, death reigned through that one man, much more will those who receive the abundance of grace and the free gift of righteousness reign in life through the one man Jesus Christ."* (Rom. 5:12,15, 17)

The original mandate bestowed on humanity at creation was to rule and have dominion over the planet. Death through the sin of one man contravened that mandate. Yeshua's death destroyed the power of death, so that in Yeshua, humanity could again *"reign in life."*

Yeshua is God's appointed ruler. Hypothetically, he could have ruled over the planet as king without fulfilling his priestly role. *"The Word was God...All things were made through him... He did not count equality with God a thing to be grasped... The earth is the LORD's and everything in it."*[89] As the Lord of glory there was nothing Yeshua was required to do to rule over that which was already his. It is only because it was his intent to bring *"many sons to glory"* that the founder of our salvation was made *"perfect through suffering. For he who sanctifies and those who are sanctified all have one source. That is why he is not ashamed to call them brothers"* (Heb. 2:10,11).

Yeshua's death was solely for our benefit. Not just so that we would be rescued from death, but even more so, that we would reign with him in life. Our rescue from death was not the ultimate goal, but rather, the necessary means to fulfill the purpose for which we were originally created: to rule.

Yeshua will be honoured and worshipped for all eternity as the Lamb that was slain - his priesthood is forever. Not only is Yeshua's death efficacious forever, but also as our "Great High Priest," he lives forever to intercede on our behalf (Heb. 7:25). It is through Yeshua's eternal priesthood that we have the assurance to draw near to God's throne (Heb. 4:16). As I stated in the introduction, priestly service was never exclusively atoning sacrifice.[90] By offering sacrifice on behalf of the people, a priest facilitated worship and communion between God and those who drew near through burnt offerings and peace offerings. Yeshua's atoning sacrifice was once and for all time (Heb. 7:27; 10:10), but as the priest who lives forever he facilitates our oneness – both as

---

[89] See, John 1:1,3; Phil. 2:6; Ps. 24:1
[90] See, footnote, p. 8

God's people together and in our communion with the Father and Son (John 17:21).

Yeshua reigns forever as God's appointed king and he lives forever as our Great High Priest. As I stated earlier, it is not my intention to pit Yeshua's priestly role against his identity as king. He has ascended to the highest place with all kingly authority because he took the lowest place in priestly service. The Lion of the tribe of Judah - the king, is the one who has prevailed, but when John looked to behold this majestic lion he saw *"a lamb standing as though it had been slain"* (Rev. 5:5-6).

His reign is forever because he is the Lord of Glory. His priestly service is eternal because as *"a priest forever after the order of Melchizedek"* (Ps. 110:4), he serves those that belong to him to facilitate their inheritance as joint heirs. When he returns we will see everything in subjection to him. But a wonder beyond all comprehension, because of his priestly service, we too will share in his reign as fellow heirs with the Messiah (Rom. 8:17).

> *"For I consider that the sufferings of this present time are not worth comparing with the glory that is to be revealed to us. For the creation waits with eager longing for the revealing of the sons of God. For the creation was subjected to futility, not willingly, but because of him who subjected it, in hope that the creation itself will be set free from its bondage to corruption and obtain the freedom of the glory of the children of God."*
> (Rom. 8:18–21)

Yeshua saved us from death to restore us to our original status as rulers on planet earth, not rulers who choose to be independent from God but rulers in Messiah. We are joint heirs with the king who was perfected for our sakes through suffering. He not only offered the sacrifice that frees us from death, he lives forever as the example of the one who received the highest place by taking the lowest place. Authority to rule over planet earth has always been Yeshua's sovereign claim. When he returns, humanity's rule is restored only in so much as we are joined to him and fellow heirs in him.

CHAPTER 10

The Dual Mandate of Israel's King

The Davidic covenant promised David that one of his heirs would rule over Israel forever (1 Chron. 17:14). Daniel's vision of the heavenly throne room revealed "*one like a son of man*" receiving an eternal kingdom over "*all peoples, nations and languages*" (Dan. 7:14). Psalm 2 clarified that the identity of the eternal ruler of Israel and the eternal ruler of all peoples, nations and languages is the same person. God's appointed ruler whose throne is in Zion (Ps. 2:6) is promised all nations as his inheritance (Ps. 2:8).

The king of Israel's inheritance of all nations is more than a reward for faithfulness. God's plan for Israel, and by extension Israel's king had always been determined with the nations in view. Israel's chosenness was a choosing on behalf of the nations.[91] The ultimate goal for God's appointed king is to restore God's authority over the whole planet. All nations and peoples are to come under Messiah's rule and banner. God's method to bring about this transformation is through the choosing of the one nation, set apart from the nations as distinct and chosen - chosen to fulfill God's will on behalf of the nations. The head of this chosen nation, Israel's king, God's appointed ruler, is the one through which God's rule is re-established over the planet. Therefore, the Messiah is both ruler of Israel and all nations. His mandate as God's appointed ruler is both to Israel and the nations,[92] and both these mandates work in complimentary fashion so that God's will on earth is done as it is in heaven.

---

[91] For further reading see, Marty Shoub, "To the Jew First." Chapter 4, "The Offence of Israel's Chosenness."

[92] I believe the term "dual mandate" was originally coined by Tikkun Ministries International Director, Asher Intrater.

This dual mandate is first expressed in Abraham's call. God promised to bless Abraham and make a great nation out of his descendants. He also promised that through Abraham (and his descendants), [93] *"all the families of the earth shall be blessed"* (Gen. 12:3). The relationship between Israel and the nations continues throughout the pages of the Hebrew Scriptures. Isaiah focused on this relationship specifically with reference to Messiah and his commission as Gods appointed ruler.

Isaiah 11 begins with a picture of a green shoot emerging out of an old stump.

"There shall come forth a shoot from the stump of Jesse, and a branch from his roots shall bear fruit." (Isa. 11:1)

The stump is the Davidic dynasty, here termed *"the stump of Jesse [David's father],"* (Isa. 11:1). A new shoot emerges out of what appears to be old and dead, revitalizing and re-establishing the dynasty. Isaiah 11:1 does not describe what type of tree had been felled to leave an old stump in the ground, but I believe Isaiah had an olive tree in view. Olive trees do not die when they are cut down. As long as the root remains alive, the tree will send forth new shoots to preserve its vitality. As long as an olive tree's root remains alive, the tree continues to live.[94] The image is clear: though it may look like the Davidic dynasty is dead, out of the old line will emerge a new king, the anointed one, on whom the Spirit of the Lord rests (Isa. 11:2).

The passage goes on to describe the characteristics of his kingdom. He will bring justice to the poor and oppressed, he will punish the wicked, and under his domain, nature will be transformed from savage "red in tooth and claw" to former prey and predator dwelling together, *"They shall not hurt or destroy in all*

---

[93] In Galatians 3:16 Paul makes a midrash on Genesis 12 focusing the fulfillment of the Abrahamic promises on his offspring singular, that is through Messiah Yeshua.

[94] This adds significance to Paul's discussion in Romans 11 about the root of the Olive tree and branches broken off.

my holy mountain; for the earth shall be full of the knowledge of the LORD *as the waters cover the sea"* (Isa. 11:9). This is a vision of the final consummation of creation under Messiah Yeshua's reign.

The passage shifts in emphasis, from the glorious final outcome to Messiah's mandate among the nations and to his own people Israel.

"And in that day there shall be a Root of Jesse, Who shall stand as a banner to the people[s]; For the Gentiles shall seek Him, And His resting place shall be glorious." It shall come to pass in that day That the Lord shall set His hand again the second time To recover the remnant of His people who are left, From Assyria and Egypt, From Pathros and Cush, From Elam and Shinar, From Hamath and the islands of the sea. He will set up a banner for the nations, And will assemble the outcasts of Israel, And gather together the dispersed of Judah From the four corners of the earth." (Isa. 11:10–12 NKJV)

The one who gathers the *"banished of Israel"* and the *"dispersed of Judah"* stands as a banner[95] for the peoples/nations. Israel's restoration results in a song of praise where the inhabitants of Zion shout for joy, because *"great in your midst is the Holy One of Israel"* (Isa. 12:6). This same company exalts the name of the LORD by making *"known His deeds among the peoples"* (Isa. 12:3).

This same pattern of Messiah both for Israel and the nations is repeated in Isaiah 49. Isaiah 49 fits within the servant passages of Isaiah. The servant passages begin with Isaiah 41:8 and end with Isaiah 53:12. Sometimes the nation of Israel is in view (Isa.41:8);[96] other servant passages refer to Israel's representative head, the Messiah. As we will explore below, in Isaiah 49 the Messiah is clearly in view. Isaiah 49 describes the purpose of Messiah's birth:

---

[95] Heb. נֵס עַמִּים (Nes Ammim)
[96] "But you Israel, my servant, Jacob whom I have chosen…"

111

"And now the LORD says, he who formed me from the womb to be his servant, to bring Jacob back to him; and that Israel might be gathered to him— for I am honored in the eyes of the LORD, and my God has become my strength— he says: 'It is too light a thing that you should be my servant to raise up the tribes of Jacob and to bring back the preserved of Israel; I will make you as a light for the nations, that my salvation may reach to the end of the earth.'" (Isa. 49:5–6)

According to Isaiah 49:5,6 the primary purpose for Messiah's birth was to restore and gather Israel back to God, and bring Israel back from exile. This echoes Isaiah 11:11,12 where Messiah will *"recover the remnant that remains of his people"* and *"will assemble the banished of Israel, and gather the dispersed of Judah from the four corners of the earth."* The Servant was formed in the womb to accomplish Israel's restoration. The Father who formed the Servant for this purpose declared that *"to raise up the tribes of Jacob and to bring back the preserved of Israel"* was not sufficient enough a task to warrant so auspicious an event as Messiah's incarnation. In order for *"The Word [to become] flesh and dwell among us,"* even Israel's restoration is not enough. Messiah was born not only for Israel's sake but for the nations as well.

The Messiah who in Isaiah 11 stands as a banner for the peoples, and as the one whom the Gentiles will seek out is described in Isaiah 49 as the *"light for the nations."*

In this passage Messiah's mandate is clearly demonstrated to accomplish a dual purpose, both for Israel and for the nations. Unfortunately, it appears that for the most part, the Body of Messiah has so stressed Messiah's mandate towards the nations that it has almost completely overshadowed his mandate for Israel. Contrary to our emphasis on salvation for the nations, according to Isaiah 49, the primary goal of Messiah's birth was to accomplish Israel's restoration.

Isaiah 49 presents Messiah's mandate for the nations as a concern for Messiah's stature and reputation. This is similar to Psalm 2's bestowal of the nations to Messiah as just recompense for his exalted position as God's chosen ruler. However, in as much as Messiah Yeshua's worthiness far surpasses any material gift or earthly status, even so, according to Isaiah 49, the same one appointed king in Psalm 2 is born as God's servant to do heaven's bidding. God's king was chosen from the beginning, not only to rule, but also as a priest to bring restoration and salvation to Israel and the nations.

The dual mandate is also expressed in terms of Yeshua's return. We will address this in detail in Part Three, where we will explore the King of Israel and the Last Days. At this juncture we will only be touching on Yeshua's return in context of the timing of this event with respect to Messiah's dual mandate. Yeshua explained that before he would return, the gospel of the kingdom had to be preached to all nations:

> *"And this gospel of the kingdom will be proclaimed throughout the whole world as a testimony to all nations, and then the end will come."* (Matt. 24:14)

Most of us are familiar with this verse as a marker that requires fulfillment before Yeshua's return. This is in keeping with the "Great Commission" which concludes all three synoptic gospels[97] (Matt. 28:19,20; Mark 16:15; Luke 24:47). The end does not come without Yeshua's mandate to the nations being fulfilled.

The Church in the nations has identified this mandate as the raison d'être for its identity and witness in the world. Certainly, as Yeshua's last command as recorded in the synoptic gospels, this directive must have a high priority for all of Yeshua's disciples.

In keeping with Messiah's mandate to restore the children of Israel, in Matthew's gospel, Yeshua added another pre-condition which required fulfillment before his return. Just before the Olivet discourse, at the end of Yeshua's pronouncement of woes on Israel's leaders he proclaimed, *"For I tell you, you will not see me*

---

[97] The Gospel of John ends with a different narrative but a similar instruction is recorded in John 20:21: *"As the Father has sent me, I also send you."*

again, until you say, 'Blessed is he who comes in the name of the Lord'" (Matt. 23:39).

In other words, *"the end"* does not come until the leaders of Jerusalem acknowledge that Yeshua is the intended recipient of this messianic benediction from Psalm 118:26. The gospel must be preached as a witness against all nations, and Israel's leadership must acknowledge Yeshua's messiahship before the end shall come. Both of Messiah's mandates are crucial to God's end time purposes and ultimately, the consummation of all things.

It is time for the Church to re-orient itself to Messiah's mandate towards Israel's restoration. The Church has embraced Messiah's mission to the nations as its own mandate. Typically, the Great Commission is understood not so much as Yeshua's mandate from Isaiah 49:5,6 but the Church's own mandate from Matthew 28:19,20.

As we had discussed above, Messiah's dual mandate is first described in Isaiah 11. According to Isaiah 11:10, Messiah *"shall stand as a banner to the people[s]; for the Gentiles shall seek Him, and His resting place shall be glorious."* Likewise, the Messiah takes the initiative to gather Israel back to the land:

> *"In that day the Lord will extend his hand yet a second time to recover the remnant that remains of his people...and will assemble the banished of Israel, and gather the dispersed of Judah from the four corners of the earth."* (Isa. 11:11–12)

The Scriptures describe Israel's restoration as Israel's return. The Scriptures do not separate the physical return of the Jewish people to the land of promise from their spiritual transformation. The promise of return is outlined in the Mosaic covenant in Deuteronomy 30. Israel's restoration is presented here as a physical return to the land from exile, and a spiritual transformation of the heart:

> *"And when all these things come upon you, the blessing and the curse, which I have set before you, and you call them to mind among all the nations where the LORD your God has driven*

114

you, and return to the LORD *your God, you and your children,*
and obey his voice in all that I command you today, with all
your heart and with all your soul, then the LORD *your God*
will restore your fortunes and have mercy on you, and he will
gather you again from all the peoples where the LORD *your*
God has scattered you. ... And the LORD *your God will*
circumcise your heart and the heart of your offspring, so that
you will love the LORD *your God with all your heart and with*
all your soul, that you may live." (Deut. 30: 1–6)

In this passage, Israel's return is predicated on Israel first
returning to the LORD with all their *"heart and soul."*[98] The LORD's
response to this repentance is to return exiled Israel back to the
land of promise. Israel's return is not completed by their physical
re-settlement in the land. Once re-gathered, the LORD promised
to *"circumcise"* Israel's heart, so as to transform the nation into
obedient children who truly love the God of Israel, obey His
commands and live.

The promise of the circumcised heart foreshadows the New
Covenant, which Jeremiah described as writing the Torah on
Israel's heart (Jer. 31:33). Jeremiah also described this spiritual
transformation as a personal, intimate relationship, and the
forgiveness and cleansing from sin, *"for they shall all know me, from*
the least of them to the greatest, declares the LORD. *For I will forgive*
their iniquity, and I will remember their sin no more" (Jer. 31:34).

The parallel passage in Ezekiel also described Israel's inner heart
transformation:

> *"And I will give you a new heart, and a new spirit I will put*
> *within you. And I will remove the heart of stone from your*
> *flesh and give you a heart of flesh. And I will put my Spirit*
> *within you, and cause you to walk in my statutes and be*
> *careful to obey my rules. You shall dwell in the land that I gave*

---

[98] Jeremiah 32:41 declares that God will plant Israel back in the land with
all His heart and soul.

to your fathers, and you shall be my people, and I will be your God." (Ezek. 36:26–29)

In the Ezekiel passage, what Deuteronomy described as "love and live" and Jeremiah described as writing the Torah on Israel's heart is described as a new heart with the result that Israel walks in God's statutes and obeys God's rules.[99] As in the Deuteronomy passage, Ezekiel's version of Israel's transformed heart is connected to Israel's physical return from exile.[100] These two elements of return are not portrayed as separate events but co-facets of Israel's return – a physical return from exile, and a spiritual return predicated on an inner transformation of the heart. Though the Deuteronomy passage requires Israel to initiate the return process through repentance, the Ezekiel passage describes the LORD as the initiator of Israel's return for the sake of His name (Ezek. 36:22-24). In both cases, Israel returns to the land and there in the land, receives a radical heart transformation.

Israel's return to the land is connected to Messiah's dual mandate, and includes specific instructions for Gentiles to participate in Israel's restoration. In Isaiah 49 these same nations who flock to Messiah's banner in Isaiah 11, are yet again summoned, this time not to rest but to do his bidding:

"Thus says the Lord GOD: "Behold, I will lift up my hand to the nations, and raise my signal[101]to the peoples; and they shall bring your sons in their arms, and your daughters shall be carried on their shoulders." (Isa. 49:22)

Isaiah 49 outlines the purpose of Messiah's birth to both restore Israel, and bring salvation to the nations. The paradigm

---

[99] "Statutes" is the ESV translation of the Hebrew, "*hoq*" (הק), often translated elsewhere as laws or ordinances. Likewise ESV has "rules" for "*mishpat*" (משפט) often translated as statutes or judgments.

[100] Jeremiah's version of Israel's transformation is also intrinsically connected to Israel's return to the land from exile. See, Jer. 31:27,28, 38-40.

[101] The Hebrew word for banner, signal or sign used in Isaiah 11:10 and Isaiah 49:22 is the same: "*nes*" (נס.)

for Israel's restoration is established through the covenant terms of Deuteronomy 30. Israel returns to the land from exile and there is given a new heart to love the LORD and live. Isaiah goes on to describe the Gentiles as the agents through whom Israel is returned back to the land.

Those first Jewish disciples moved their priorities beyond just the restoration of their own people, so as to bring Messiah's salvation to all nations, even to the ends of the earth. So now, at the end of the age, God is beckoning to His people in the nations, the ones who first received God's salvation through the witness and sacrifice of Jewish believers, to engage in returning the Jewish people back to the land, and ultimately to their spiritual restoration. In as much as the gospel to all nations is Messiah's mandate and therefore the mandate of all of Messiah's followers, so too Messiah's mandate to restore the tribes of Jacob is also the mandate of all Messiah's disciples.

Part 3

The King of Israel and the Consummation of All Things

CHAPTER 11

The End and the Beginning

One cannot consider the Last Days without considering the beginning of days. The Last Days is the final chapter in bringing all things together, completing the redemption of creation and ultimately, bringing about the consummation of all things. The consummation is the final outcome of God's plan and purpose for creation. In western culture, consummation is specifically related to marriage. This is a very good picture of the final consummation. A man and woman exchange vows and symbols of their fidelity, they sign legal documents binding them to their new marital status, but it is only with their sexual union that the marriage is consummated. Despite all the movement towards their oneness, it is only with the act that makes them "one flesh" that they are truly married. As Paul explained, this is a picture between Messiah and the church (Eph. 5:32). The consummation of all things is a uniting of Messiah and his bride. It is a becoming one that only currently is enjoyed together by Father and Son (John 17:21).

In some ways, the final outcome of things is a return to the idyllic circumstances of the beginning. When Isaiah prophesied that the Leopard and the goat [102] would lie down together (Isa. 11:6), he was alluding to the peaceful harmony between animals that existed in Eden. Isaiah 11 also describes harmony between humans and all animals, even predators and harmful

---

[102] African friends have explained to me that whereas a lion that entered a goat pen would kill a goat and eat it, a leopard in the same circumstances would not only eat a goat to satisfy its hunger but it would kill every last animal for sport. This adds emphasis to the profound transition of leopards and goats lying down together.

creatures (Isa. 11:6,8). This hearkens back to all the animals coming before Adam in order to receive their name from him (Gen. 2:19,20).

Sometimes Eden is considered a perfect world. This was not the case. Though ideal in every respect, there were anticipated conditions not yet fulfilled in Eden, and therefore it was not yet perfect. Mankind was given the directive to *"fill the earth and subdue it"* (Gen. 1:28). This implies that the will of heaven was not fully realized across the planet because human beings, God's regents over the creation were not yet in place across the globe.

The first petition in Yeshua's paradigm prayer for his followers is, *"Your kingdom come, your will be done on earth as it is in heaven"* (Matt. 6:10). The request for God's will done on earth in the same way it is done in heaven is a recognition of the rebellion currently opposing God's will on planet earth. However, it also hearkens to an expectation that had yet to be realized prior to the fall. Humanity had not yet spread out across the globe. The will of God for mankind to have dominion had not yet been exercised in every region of the planet. In the final consummation of all things, redeemed humanity under the headship of Messiah will extend God's rule and will to every facet of the global domain.

Two trees were highlighted in Eden, the tree of the knowledge of good and evil and the tree of life (Gen. 2:9). The prohibition against eating was only for the tree of the knowledge of good and evil. This presumes that at some point, Adam and Eve were to partake of the tree of life. If according to the divine plan they only did the will of their Heavenly Father, this would have been at the appropriate time. It is also possible that at some point in their development, Adam and Eve would have had the prohibition against partaking of the tree of the knowledge of good and evil lifted. Was the tree there only to serve as a testing point of obedience or did it have an additional function and purpose?[103]

---

[103] Though the tree of the knowledge of good and evil did serve as a testing point for human obedience to God's will I consider it possible, that it also had further purpose. As part of the very good creation it was made according to the good and perfect will of our Heavenly Father. Of course,

We can only speculate about this scenario. Because they rebelled against heaven's will by partaking of the tree of the knowledge of good and evil, their access to partaking of the tree of life was removed (Gen. 3:22-24). In the consummation, access to the tree of life will be restored to humanity (Rev. 2:7; 22:14).

The disaster that was the fall was precipitated by human rebellion to the will of God. It was also a deception conceived and executed by Satan, the leader of an angelic rebellion that appears to predate the creation of the world. The Scriptures do not provide enough specific details to know exactly when this angelic rebellion took place,[104] but it is presumed in the Scriptures that one purpose for humanity's creation was to function as the judges of the rebellious heavenly beings:

"What is man that you are mindful of him, and the son of man that you care for him? Yet you have made him a little lower than the heavenly beings and crowned him with glory and honor. You have given him dominion over the works of your hands; you have put all things under his feet" (Ps. 8:4–6)

The writer of Hebrews quotes this verse and adds, *"Now in putting everything in subjection to him, he left nothing outside his control"* (Heb. 2:8). This presumes *"the heavenly beings"* are also under the Son of Man's feet. The writer is specifically referring to Yeshua. However, Paul admonished the Corinthians for going to public law courts explaining to them, *"Do you not know that we are to judge angels?"* (1 Cor. 6:3). Yeshua is the head of redeemed humanity and those who belong to him will share in his authority and rule (Rev. 2:26,27).

Therefore there are three components of the consummation that were not realized at creation. 1. The earth was not populated

---

this is speculation on my part. I hope the reader will not read too much into my musing on this matter.

[104] The angelic rebellion that led to an angelic being know has the adversary, Hebrew: *ha satan* (השטן), could have taken place at any time prior to creation or within the "6 days" of the creation process. It is beyond the scope of this book to consider this matter beyond a cursory investigation.

throughout all its regions, and therefore the rule of God through humanity was not completely exercised across the globe. The creation was not yet under humanity's dominion. 2. Humanity had not yet partaken of the tree of life, and therefore had not entered into a glorified state. 3. The rebellious heavenly powers had not yet been judged. There remained injustice within creation, even if prior to the fall it did not directly touch humanity. These divine intentions had not yet been realized. With the consummation of all things not only will creation experience the idyllic features of the original creation, but also redeemed humanity in Messiah will truly have dominion over the planet, will partake of the tree of life and judge all evil agents, even those heavenly beings who left their own positions of authority (Jude 6).

The central actor in all this is of course Yeshua, God's appointed ruler. In Yeshua, all of the Father's purposes will be realized, including restoring humanity back into the proper place of rulership as the Father originally intended. In the beginning the ruler mandate was given to Adam and Eve. We can only speculate as to how humanity's rule over the planet would have been realized to the consummation if Yeshua had not been required to act in priestly intercession to restore the creation order. After the fall it was necessary for the divine son to become flesh, the seed of the woman, in order to restore creation as the new representative head of humanity.

This places Yeshua's priestly atonement within the context of the creation mandate. Yeshua's saving act was not an end in itself but the necessary redemptive means to complete humanity's restoration and provide the way forward for humanity's consummation. This does not diminish the glory of Yeshua's priestly ministry but it helps us to shift our focus to see salvation as more than simply a saving from sin and death, but also the reigning in life towards the final consummation.

In John's vision of the heavenly courtroom he saw *"in the right hand of him who was seated on the throne a scroll written within and on the back, sealed with seven seals"* (Rev. 5:1). An angel cried out, *"Who is worthy to open the scroll and break its seals?"* (Rev. 5:2). The question is not really about who can open the scroll and read its contents but who can open the scroll and release the final purposes of God contained within the scroll.[105] John began to weep, *"because no one was found worthy to open the scroll or look into it"* (Rev. 5:3). The final end time purposes of God, the judgments and acts that bring about the final consummation were held in abeyance until one could be found who was worthy to open the sealed scroll.

It appeared as if there was no one in both heaven and earth that had the authority and qualifications necessary to release the final consummation purposes. John wept because if the scroll was not opened, if the divine pronouncements were not released, then all of God's purposes ground to a halt, all that had taken place up to that moment was in vain and of no consequence if the final chapter did not unfold.

One of the angelic elders reassured John, *"Weep no more; behold, the Lion of the tribe of Judah, the Root of David, has conquered, so that he can open the scroll and its seven seals"* (Rev. 5:5). The only being within heaven and earth that had the authority and qualifications to open the scroll was *"the Lion of the tribe of Judah,"* the king of Israel, Yeshua the Messiah.

God's appointed ruler is worthy to open the scroll because he has received the Father's authority to rule over all nations (Ps. 2:8; Dan. 7:14) and because he *"has conquered."* Within the Father's purposes to redeem mankind, the one appointed to rule entered into his authority in the highest place by taking the lowest place, suffering and dying as a priest after the order of Melchizedek.

In order to bring *"many sons to glory,"* the Father determined to *"make the founder of their salvation perfect through suffering"* (Heb. 2:10). Yeshua *"was declared to be the Son of God in power according to the Spirit of holiness by his resurrection from the dead"* (Rom. 1:4). The redeemer, who died on behalf of all and was raised from the dead to the highest place, is the conqueror of

---

[105] David E. Aune, "Revelation" (Word Biblical Commentary 52A; Waco, TX: Word, Inc. 1997), 346.

death and all powers. He is worthy to fulfill God's final consummation purposes. That is why, when John turned to behold the Lion of the Tribe of Judah he saw *"a lamb standing, as though it had been slain"* (Rev. 5:6).

Yeshua is the king/priest who brings in the final consummation. His priesthood is universal, by his blood he *"ransomed people for God from every tribe and language and people and nation, and [he has] made them a kingdom and priests to our God, and they shall reign on the earth"* (Rev. 5:9–10). But his kingship is specific; he is the Lion of the tribe of Judah, the king of Israel. Too often, consideration of the End-Times minimizes Yeshua's return with respect to the land of Israel and the Jewish people. As we will explore in the next chapter, Yeshua's return has everything to do with Israel, Jerusalem and the Jewish people.

CHAPTER 12

The City of the Great King

"But I say to you, do not take an oath at all, either by heaven, for it is the throne of God, or by the earth, for it is his footstool, or by Jerusalem, for it is the city of the great King."
(Matt. 5:34–35)

Planet earth in the world to come will echo many features of the earth as it was at creation. The final scene within the Scriptures is the description of the New Jerusalem, the abode where God will dwell with mankind forever (Rev. 21:3,4).

It is noteworthy that from Abraham through David, and Solomon to Yeshua, the most significant events in biblical history took place at Jerusalem. Jerusalem is where Abraham and the kings of Canaan met Melchizedek (Gen.14:17,18). Melchizedek (lit. king of righteousness) was king of Salem (Hebrew, *Shalem* (שלם), that is, king of peace[106]. Jerusalem was where Abraham bound his son Isaac for sacrifice (Gen. 22:2). Jerusalem was David's capital (2 Sam. 5:5), Jerusalem was the site of Solomon's Temple (2 Chron. 3:1), and Jerusalem was the site of Yeshua's death and resurrection.

The tree of Life that stood in the Garden of Eden will again appear in the New Jerusalem (Rev. 22:2). Just as the LORD God walked in the cool of the garden with Adam and Eve (Gen. 3:8), so in the New Jerusalem, God will dwell with mankind forever.

---

[106] In Modern Hebrew Jerusalem is *Yerushalyim* (ירושלים), but in the Scriptures, this variant spelling is only used 5 times. In over 700 other references the city is called *Yerushalem* (ירושלם) that is, "Foundation of Peace."

Asher Intrater, in his book, *Alignment* wrote, "Eden and Jerusalem have always been one." [107] Intrater explains the correspondence between Eden and Jerusalem, "Yeshua was crucified on the Tree in the same place where the sin on the tree was committed. Yeshua was raised from the earth where Adam was made from the earth. Yeshua's sacrifice and the sacrifices of Solomon's Temple and the sacrifice of Isaac are all in Jerusalem."[108]

The geography of Eden also provides a clue to suggest that Eden's former location corresponds to biblical and present day Jerusalem. Genesis 2 described four rivers flowing out from the midst of the garden:

> *"A river flowed out of Eden to water the garden, and there it divided and became four rivers. The name of the first is the Pishon. It is the one that flowed around the whole land of Havilah, where there is gold...The name of the second river is the Gihon. It is the one that flowed around the whole land of Cush. And the name of the third river is the Tigris, which flows east of Assyria. And the fourth river is the Euphrates."* (Gen. 2:10–14)

Two of the rivers mentioned, the Euphrates and Tigris rivers are well known to the present day. They both flow out of Eastern Turkey across Mesopotamia into the Persian Gulf. We no longer know the location of the other two rivers, the Gihon and the Pishon. We do have some clues as to their possible whereabouts.

The Pishon *"flowed around the whole land of Havilah."* The word "Havilah" (חוילה), is etymologically related to the Hebrew word for sand (*Khool,* חול). Havilah could be understood to mean sand land, most likely Arabia[109]. The second river named, the Gihon *"flowed around the whole land of Cush."* Cush is often understood to mean Ethiopia but more accurately would be the

---

[107] Asher Intrater. Alignment" (Frederick, MD: Revive Israel Media, 2017), 216

[108] Ibid.

[109] BDB, p. 296

Nile lands south of Egypt, equivalent to modern Sudan and South Sudan[110].

The map below sets out the current placement of the Euphrates and Tigris rivers and the potential identity of the Pishon and Gihon rivers. It is likely that the Gihon is identified with the Nile or the White Nile River and the Pishon is perhaps the Blue Nile or some other now extinct ancient waterway, east of the Nile and south of Mesopotamia. Either way, in the midst of these four rivers is the land of Israel, and centrally located in the heart of the nation, is the city of Jerusalem.

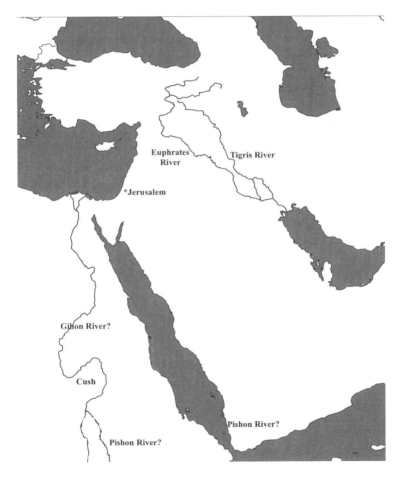

[110] BDB, p. 161

Aside from Jerusalem's geographical proximity to these rivers, Jerusalem's water source also bears the same name as the river that flowed out of the garden through Cush (Gihon, 2 Chron. 32:30). Further, the prophetic Scriptures anticipate rivers will again flow from Jerusalem (See, Zech.14:8; Ezek. 47:1; Joel 3:18).

The geographical evidence by itself is compelling but not quite firm enough for geographic certainty. However, taken together with all the significant events that have taken place in Israel's history, the "Gihon" spring at Jerusalem, the prophetic anticipation of rivers flowing from Jerusalem, and the prophetic centrality of Jerusalem in the age to come, the argument for Eden being once, where Jerusalem now is, has strong evidentiary support.

Even putting aside past events and the connection of Jerusalem to Eden, the prophetic future orientation of the last days is centered on Jerusalem. After Yeshua's resurrection he taught his disciples for forty days about the kingdom of God (Acts 1:3). At the conclusion of Yeshua's teaching, on their last meeting together, the disciples asked him, *"Lord, will you at this time restore the kingdom to Israel?"* (Acts 1:6).

Some have suggested that this question arose out of the disciples' expectation of seats of authority in Israel's restored kingdom[111] (Matt. 19:18). Later in the chapter we learn that this discourse took place on the Mt of Olives (Acts 1:12). A better explanation for their inquiry is the location of this final meeting with Yeshua. The prophet Zechariah had foretold that at Israel's dire hour, surrounded by enemies, the Lord would bring the final victory for Israel when *"his feet shall stand on the Mount of Olives"* (Zech. 14:4). Previously they had not understood that the Messiah had to suffer to enter into his glory (Luke 24:25,26), but now here was the risen Messiah standing on the Mount of Olives just as Zechariah had prophesied. Surely, now the kingdom would be restored to Israel.

---

[111] F.F. Bruce. "The Book of Acts" (NICNT, Grand Rapids, MI: Eerdmans, 1986). 38.

Yeshua's answer was not a direct "no." Rather, he told them not to concern themselves over the timing of matters solely within the Father's domain. Instead, Yeshua refocused their attention to a more immediate priority:

> *"But you will receive power when the Holy Spirit has come upon you, and you will be my witnesses in Jerusalem and in all Judea and Samaria, and to the end of the earth."* (Acts 1:8)

In popular Christian culture the four geographic areas mentioned in Yeshua's final instructions correspond to four evangelical spheres of responsibility: Jerusalem, one's home environs; Judea, one's surrounding communities; Samaria, one's surrounding territories; ends of the earth, the international arena.[112] This is a helpful model to pursue evangelism but does not accurately reflect the priority of the command. Jerusalem was not first because it was the hometown of the disciples or for that matter of their master. They were all Galileans. Jerusalem was the priority for witness because of Jerusalem's centrality to the purposes of God.

Though Yeshua did not restore the kingdom at that moment, his departure to the right hand of the Father did correspond to the disciples' expectations based on the prophesy in Zechariah 14. Yeshua ascended to heaven from the Mount of Olives because it is to the Mount of Olives that he will return:

> *"And while they were gazing into heaven as he went, behold, two men stood by them in white robes, and said, "Men of Galilee, why do you stand looking into heaven? This Jesus, who was taken up from you into heaven, will come in the same way as you saw him go into heaven."* (Acts 1:10–11)

---

[112] Chuck Smith. "Sermon notes for Acts 1:8." Accessed April 16, 2018. https://www.blueletterbible.org/Comm/smith_chuck/SermonNotes_Act/Act_10.cfm

Yeshua will return to the Mount of Olives because his return corresponds exactly to Zechariah's prophecy. The Mount of Olives is just east across the Kidron Valley from Jerusalem. According to Zechariah 14, the Lord's feet will stand on the Mount of Olives, because starting from this location he will go out to destroy Israel's enemies.

More specifically, he will go out to fight against those nations that have surrounded Jerusalem to destroy it:

> *"Behold, a day is coming for the* LORD, *when the spoil taken from you will be divided in your midst. For I will gather all the nations against Jerusalem to battle, and the city shall be taken and the houses plundered and the women raped. Half of the city shall go out into exile, but the rest of the people shall not be cut off from the city. Then the* LORD *will go out and fight against those nations as when he fights on a day of battle. On that day his feet shall stand on the Mount of Olives that lies before Jerusalem on the east, and the Mount of Olives shall be split in two... Then the* LORD *my God will come, and all the holy ones with him."* (Zech. 14:1–5)

We will address most of the elements of Zechariah's version of Yeshua's return in the next chapter. For now, the important truth is that Yeshua returns to Jerusalem and Jerusalem is the focal point of the final battle before the establishment of his kingdom on earth.

In popular culture the term "Armageddon" is synonymous with apocalyptic cataclysm. For most Christians, the "Battle of Armageddon" is understood to be the final battle between Messiah and Antichrist depicted in the book of Revelation. The word "Armageddon" is the English transliteration of the Greek word, (*Harmagedōn*, Αρμαγεδών). This in turn is a Greek transliteration of the Hebrew words (Har Megiddo, מגדו הר), that is, Mount Megiddo.

Megiddo is one the most important cities in the Ancient Near East. It lies at the northern head of the main pass through the

Carmel range at the southern end of the Jezreel Valley. Megiddo is not a natural mountain; it is a tel, a man-made hill usually built over a natural hill or rise in the land. Even today one can look out from the top of Megiddo over a large expanse in every direction. It is an ideal location for a fortress. Megiddo was (and still is), situated at a major crossroads. From this location any movement passing between the great centers of civilization in Mesopotamia and Egypt could be controlled. It was the site of many battles because whoever controlled the pass controlled the trade route. The great powers of the Hittite kingdom, Egypt, Assyria, and Babylon all fought here in order to establish control over the trade routes through Canaan. Further, its location is also conducive to the assembling of large armies.[113]

Despite Armageddon's extensive battlefield history, contrary to popular belief, the book of Revelation does not describe or refer to "the Battle of Armageddon." In Revelation 16, after the sixth bowl is poured out, John described a vision of demonic spirits *"coming out of dragon and out of the mouth of the beast and out of the mouth of the false prophet"* (Rev. 16:13). These spirits go out to deceive *"the kings of the whole world, to assemble for the battle on the great day of God the Almighty...And they assembled them at the place that in Hebrew is called Armageddon"* (Rev. 16:14,16).

It is understandable that many commentators have assumed that if the kings of the earth are gathered at Armageddon, then that is where the battle will take place. Revelation 16:14 describes the demonic forces deceiving the kings of the earth to assemble for battle. Revelation 16:16 states that the kings of the earth were assembled *"at the place that in Hebrew is called Armageddon."*

To be clear, what the scripture describes is the kings of the earth gathering at Armageddon; it does not say specifically that the final battle takes place there. Perhaps the best way to understand Armageddon's connection to the last battle is to consider the analogy of invaders establishing a beachhead to muster troops and gather supplies before striking out against the

---

[113] The last great battle at Megiddo was fought near the end of WWI between the allied forces led by the British, and the Ottoman Turks.

133

intended target. In the same way that the allied invasion of Normandy was a beachhead towards invading Germany, and especially Berlin, so the kings of the earth will gather together at Armageddon with the intent of conquering Jerusalem.

Whatever occurs at Megiddo, it is not the final battle between Messiah and antichrist. The final battle takes place at Jerusalem, some 100 kilometers to the south of Megiddo. This is clear when one compares the description of the final battle in Revelation 19 with the description of the same battle in Zechariah 14. Both passages describe the same event (we will consider this in detail in chapter 13). Revelation 19 does not indicate where the King of kings fights against the beast and the kings of the earth. Zechariah 14 is clear that the battle takes place at Jerusalem.

As I mentioned above, Jerusalem has always been the key location in God's restorative purposes. It is the seat of authority for God's appointed ruler - the city of the great king. As we will explore in our next chapter, the issue around this final battle is the ultimate authority on planet earth. Do the "kings of the earth" in league with the antichrist have authority over the planet or does God's appointed ruler have the authority over planet earth? As Psalm 2 made clear, it is God's appointed ruler whose throne is established on God's holy hill of Zion, who will receive all nations and the ends of the earth as his inheritance.

Yeshua's return is foremost to restore God's order and rule over planet earth. God's appointed ruler returns to finally quash all rebellion at the location where the rebellion started in the first place.

Jerusalem, the city of the great king is that place. As we shall see, Jerusalem also serves as the geopolitical marker proclaiming planet earth as the property of YHVH, the God of Israel, the Creator of the universe.

CHAPTER 13

The King's Return and the Ruling Powers

"The oracle of the word of the LORD *concerning Israel: Thus declares the* LORD, *who stretched out the heavens and founded the earth and formed the spirit of man within him: "Behold, I am about to make Jerusalem a cup of staggering to all the surrounding peoples. The siege of Jerusalem will also be against Judah. On that day I will make Jerusalem a heavy stone for all the peoples. All who lift it will surely hurt themselves. And all the nations of the earth will gather against it."* (Zech. 12:1–3)

In chapter 6 I wrote, "The pattern of rebellion that started with Adam and Eve continues on in us all, but in a unique way with respect to how human beings have organized themselves to rule over nations. Psalm 2:1-3 portrays the nations in a raging rebellion against God's rule. The psalm identifies the leaders of these nations as *The Kings of the earth.* Over the course of time Adam and Eve's decision to choose for themselves expanded into the international arena and like Adam and Eve, the international leaders refused to heed the Creator's instructions." [114] This rebellion is also directed against the Creator's anointed king – the Messiah.

The raging of the kings of the earth described in Psalm 2 finds its ultimate expression in the Last Days. The kings of the earth join the spiritual powers opposed to the God of Israel and His Messiah, and set out to destroy Jerusalem, *"the city of the*

---

[114] P.77 above

great King" (Ps. 48:2; Matt. 5:35). Consideration of Jerusalem summons deeply held political opinions but the decision to attack Jerusalem at the heart of it, is not about fulfilling secular, political aspirations. Jerusalem is the target of animus because of what it represents in God's purposes and plans.

The kings of the earth follow the rebellion of Adam by refusing to submit to God's rule, choosing instead to be the final arbitrators of what is right and wrong. Sometimes, these rulers have had good intentions, but ultimately they have still refused to comply with the will of heaven. Israel, and especially Jerusalem is the focal point of so much contention, because it is the geo-political marker exposing humanity's rebellion against the Creator. The Creator has established Jerusalem *"as a heavy stone for all peoples"* (Zech. 12:3).

In the Scriptures, a stone or a pillar serves as a memorial witness to the people (Gen. 31:45; 1 Sam. 7:12). It is a visible signpost that communicates a message to the present community, and endures as such to bear witness to future generations. Zechariah 12:3 depicts the city of Jerusalem as such a stone. The presence of Jerusalem on planet earth is a visible witness to all peoples that the God of Israel is the creator of heaven and earth. It is no wonder that those opposed to the God of Israel seek to remove this witness against them.

As Zechariah 12:3 goes on to say, though they might try and remove this stone, they will never succeed because it was laid by God's own hand: *"All who lift it will surely hurt themselves. And all the nations of the earth will gather against it."* God's solution to the raging of the kings of the earth was to establish His appointed king on His holy hill of Zion (Ps. 2:6). Jerusalem stands as witness to the kings of the earth that they are not the final decision makers regarding the rule over the nations of the world. Their choice is not the final word. Rather, the Creator has established His own king to rule over the planet. He will do the maker's bidding and his throne will be established in Jerusalem.

The Christian worldview usually considers the matter of sin and rebellion as solely an individual, personal matter. People are sinners and every person will have to give an account of their own choices and actions to the Creator. The Scriptures hold individuals to account, but more often pronounce judgments on nations and groups of people. Not only individuals will give an account, but also nations will be judged before God's throne.

The well-known parable of the sheep and the goats depicted in Matthew 25, is usually cast in terms of our personal response to those who are suffering life's depravations. "Did I visit prisoners and the infirm?" "Did I consider the poor?" "Did I aid those who are suffering?" These are important questions. Our responsibility to individuals in need is clearly explained in the parable of the Good Samaritan, and summed up in the second greatest command, *"you shall love your neighbor as yourself"* (Lev. 19:18).

In the parable of the sheep and the goats, Yeshua explained that when he returns to sit on his throne of glory, *"All the nations will be gathered before Him, and He will separate them one from another, as a shepherd divides his sheep from the goats"* (Matt. 25:32 NKJV). Here Yeshua is describing the event already prophesied by the prophet Joel:[115]

"For behold, in those days and at that time, when I restore the fortunes of Judah and Jerusalem, I will gather all the nations and bring them down to the Valley of Jehoshaphat. And I will enter into judgment with them there, on behalf of my people and my heritage Israel." (Joel 3:1–2)

The judgment of the sheep and the goats is a judgment of nations, not individuals. Yeshua will gather *"all the nations"* before him. In the Matthean description of the judgment, it is those nations described as sheep that are commended, and those nations described as goats that are punished. They are both judged on the basis of how they treated those Yeshua described as, *"the least of these my brothers."* In Joel's version of the judgment, the issue under consideration is how the nations treated God's people Israel:

---

[115] Johannes Facius. "Hastening the Coming of the Messiah." (Kent, England: Sovereign World Ltd. 2001) 51.

"And I will enter into judgment with them there, on behalf of my people and my heritage Israel, because they have scattered them among the nations and have divided up my land, and have cast lots for my people, and have traded a boy for a prostitute, and have sold a girl for wine and have drunk it." (Joel 3:2–3)

Yeshua's description of the judgment of the nations in Matthew 25 equates *"the least of these my brethren"* with Joel's *"my people and my heritage Israel."* When Yeshua returns to rule, the nations will give an account to him with respect to his people, the nation of Israel. This is not to say that there will be no accountability for how Christians have faired under the rule of nations. One could reasonably make the argument that the least of Yeshua's brethren also includes those Gentiles who belong to him.

For the purpose of our discussion, the critical issue is that nations, not just individuals will be held to account. Sometimes nations are considered to be a human contrivance, a practical, political structure that human beings have created to organize themselves. But nations[116] have a divine structure to them. As I described in chapter 5, God is the author of national boundaries and national destinies.[117]

The description in Zechariah of all the nations gathered in opposition to Jerusalem, is not so much a political difference of opinion between the political leaders of Israel and the political leaders of the nations, but a witness against the nations and their rulers. It is an indictment against the kings of the earth, demonstrating to all, that they are in rebellion against the ultimate authority on planet earth, the LORD and his Messiah.

Yeshua will judge the nations with respect to Israel, not just because they are the apple of his eye (Zech. 2:8), but more so because Israel, and especially Jerusalem, is that geo-political

---

[116] By nations I mean not only nation states but people groups as well.
[117] See pages 63-66 above.

marker that serves as witness to all nations that the planet belongs to God, and that He has appointed His designated king to rule over all the nations from Jerusalem.

There are many reasons why God loves the Jewish people. There are many valid reasons why they have an inherent right to live in the land of Israel. Israel was chosen on behalf of the nations to serve as priests, God's representatives to all the nations of the world. But ultimately, at least within the geo-political realm, Israel serves as a witness against the rebellion of the nations, and an affirmation that the planet still belongs to God.

One could reasonably say that God's choosing of Israel is not so much about His affection for Israel, as it is about the rule of God on planet earth. Israel is that national witness to the whole planet that God the Creator, and therefore ultimate authority over planet earth is also the author of nations, the determiner of their boundaries and destinies, and He has so ordered and arranged the nations in relation to *"the number of the children of Israel."*[118]

Therefore, at the end of the age, right before Yeshua's return to rule over the planet, the Scriptures foretell that all nations will gather together to attack Jerusalem. The battle for Jerusalem is described in detail in Zechariah 14. The passage begins in Zechariah 12, where the God of Israel presents His credentials, giving Him the authority to determine the final outcomes for Israel and the nations because He is the Creator of all:

"The oracle of the word of the LORD concerning Israel: Thus declares the LORD, who stretched out the heavens and founded the earth and formed the spirit of man within him." (Zech. 12:1)

The final confrontation between the Creator and the kings of the earth occurs at Jerusalem because Jerusalem represents the sovereign Creator's designs for all nations. The Creator endued

---

[118] See discussion on the connection between Acts 17:26-28 and Deuteronomy 32:8 p. 65ff. above.

humanity with the ability and mandate to govern the planet – but as delegated rulers under His authority. With humanity's rebellion against that authority, the Creator intervened within human affairs to establish His chosen ruler as king over the planet, the king of Israel who receives all nations as his inheritance.

It is not my intention to give an account of how the details of the Last Days will unfold. Many have undertaken to describe potential scenarios related to world events. It is my view that the value of this sort of speculation is limited. However, there are a few details of which we can be certain. We know where and how the Lord will return. As the disciples were gazing upward watching Yeshua's ascent into heaven, two angels appeared to them to explain what according to the prophet Zechariah, they should have already known:

> *"Men of Galilee, why do you stand looking into heaven? This Jesus, who was taken up from you into heaven, will come in the same way as you saw him go into heaven."* (Acts 1:11)

Yeshua will return by descending onto the Mount of Olives, east of Jerusalem. This is also what Zechariah foretold:

> *"Then the LORD will go out and fight against those nations as when he fights on a day of battle. On that day his feet shall stand on the Mount of Olives that lies before Jerusalem on the east."* (Zech. 14:3–4)

The attack on Jerusalem not only serves as the flash point to end the rebellion of nations, it is also the crisis that serves to ultimately reveal the Messiah to all Israel.

> *"And on that day I will seek to destroy all the nations that come against Jerusalem. And I will pour out on the house of David and the inhabitants of Jerusalem a spirit of grace and pleas for mercy, so that, when they look on me, on him whom they have pierced, they shall mourn for him, as one mourns for*

an only child, and weep bitterly over him, as one weeps over a firstborn." (Zech. 12:9–10)

Yeshua's return confronts the nations in their rebellion against the Creator, and at the same time, confronts Israel in its rebellion against their own Messiah. This dual confrontation has very different outcomes for Israel and the nations. According to Zechariah 14:3, when Yeshua appears on the Mount of Olives, *"the LORD will go out and fight against those nations as when he fights on a day of battle."* Yeshua's return brings judgment against the nations.

At the same time, Yeshua's return holds Israel to account for their failure to recognize their own Messiah. But this accounting does not end with judgment but with salvation. In chapter four I wrote, "As God's son over the nation of Israel, the king's behavior was the primary factor determining the nation's prosperity. As we shall later explore, Israel's Messiah king will secure Israel's ultimate destiny."[119] The obedience or disobedience of Israel's kings determined how the nation fared. With respect to Yeshua, the outcome for the nation can only be blessing. Because of Yeshua's obedience as Israel's king, despite his own people failing to recognize the day of their visitation, in the end, the outcome for the nation will be salvation. This is an act of grace based on Yeshua's merits as Israel's king. Just as in times past the God of Israel spared Judah and Jerusalem for the sake of King David (2 Kings 8:19; 19:34), so at the final battle Yeshua, the Lord of Glory and King of Israel will save all Israel (Rom. 11:26).

Yeshua's return is not the beginning of judgment for Israel (as it is for the nations), but the end of judgment. The millennia long history of suffering for the Jewish people ends with Yeshua's reappearance, and the Jewish people's recognition of his true identity. The *"spirit of grace and pleas for mercy"* poured out on the Jewish people is answered with a grace to see Yeshua as the one whom they have pierced. This is a great day of deliverance but

---

[119] P. 63

also a day of mourning and contrition. Israel will *"weep bitterly over him."*

This mourning is compared to *"the mourning at[120] Haddad Rimmon in the plains of Megiddo"* (Zech. 12:11 NKJV). The reference to Haddad Rimmon is uncertain.[121] In context, this appears to be a reference to the mourning first instituted at Megiddo (presumably at Haddad Rimmon), by Jeremiah for King Josiah (2 Chron. 35:25).

Of Josiah the Scriptures record:

> *"Before him there was no king like him, who turned to the LORD with all his heart and with all his soul and with all his might, according to all the Law of Moses, nor did any like him arise after him."* (2 Kings 23:25)

Unlike all the kings who came before him there is no censure against Josiah's character in the Scriptures.[122] His one failure was to assume he had authority over Pharaoh Necho, by attempting to thwart his advance against the king of Assyria at Megiddo (2 Kings 23:29). As exemplary as he was, Josiah was not the son of David who would receive authority over the nations. He did not have the God-given authority to command Pharaoh to turn back from battle. For his presumption Josiah was killed by a seemingly random arrow strike (2 Chron. 35:22,23).

Jeremiah *"uttered a lament for Josiah; and all the singing men and singing women have spoken of Josiah in their laments to this day"*

---

[120] Some translations say "for Haddad Rimmon"(ESV). The Hebrew does not directly supply a preposition for Haddad Rimmon, "כְּמִסְפַּד הֲדַד־רִמּוֹן" *lit. "like wailing haddad rimon."*

[121] Ralph L. Smith "Micah-Malachi" (Word Biblical Commentary Vol. 32; Waco, TX: Word, Inc. 1997.). Smith suggests that the names *Ben-Hadad* (1Ki. 20:1) and *Hadadrezer* (2 Sam. 8:5), "probably refers to the god Hadad." p.278

[122] Even the great king Hezekiah failed God's test when motivated by pride he showcased his treasures to the envoys from Babylon (2 Chron. 32:31 cf. 2 Kings 20:12-15).

(2 Chron. 35:25). Josiah was not the son of David Israel had been waiting for; he was not the son given authority over all nations (Ps. 2:6-8). Jeremiah and all Israel lamented over this righteous king, perhaps even lamenting that though he demonstrated messianic traits by his zeal for the Torah and his obedience to God, he was not the Messiah.

When Israel mourns at Yeshua's return it will be similar to the mourning for Josiah. At Haddad Rimmon they mourned because the one they thought was the Messiah was in fact not the Messiah. With the mourning over Yeshua, Israel will mourn because the one they thought was not the Messiah is in fact the Messiah. In keeping with the spirit of grace and pleas for mercy, Israel will mourn in deep repentance over their grievous long-standing error of failing to receive their own king.

Yeshua's descent upon the Mount of Olives to vanquish the nations surrounding the city is also the momentous revelation of the Messiah to the Jewish people. They will look upon the one *"whom they have pierced."* Yeshua will descend to put down the rebellion of nations. The final expression of that rebellion is all nations attacking Jerusalem. There are multiple reasons why Yeshua will return, but the most direct reason, in context of the world events unfolding at that time is to rescue Jerusalem from all the nations that are attacking the city. Yeshua returns to literally save all Israel. The saviour who will defend the city is none other than the one whom was pierced on a Roman cross two millennia ago.

This same scenario is described in the book of Revelation:

> *"And I saw the beast and the kings of the earth with their armies gathered to make war against him who was sitting on the horse and against his army. And the beast was captured, and with it the false prophet who in its presence had done the signs by which he deceived those who had received the mark of the beast and those who worshiped its image. These two were thrown alive into the lake of fire that burns with sulfur. And the rest were slain by the sword that came from the mouth of*

him who was sitting on the horse, and all the birds were gorged with their flesh." (Rev. 19:19–21)

The description of all armies gathered against Jerusalem, and the LORD's feet touching the top of the Mount of Olives as He goes out to vanquish this multi-national force, is the same scenario of the Beast and the Kings of the earth gathered with their armies to make war on the King of Kings seated on his white horse. These kings of the earth had previously been warned, *"Now therefore, O kings, be wise; be warned, O rulers of the earth. Serve the LORD with fear, and rejoice with trembling. Kiss the Son, lest he be angry, and you perish in the way, for his wrath is quickly kindled"* (Ps. 2:10–12). God's word to them is *"kiss the Son,"* submit to God's authority. As Psalm 2 promised, *"Blessed are all who take refuge in him"* (Ps. 2:12).

Rather than submit to God's ruler, these kings of the earth submit to the Beast, a satanically inspired counterfeit Messiah. Their goal is to remove the *"heavy stone"* that is Jerusalem, God's geo-political marker signifying that He is indeed the Creator/Owner of the planet. If Jerusalem were to be destroyed, than the word of God would be made null and of no effect. Destroying Jerusalem would not only be an act of defiance; it would be a claim to sovereignty over the planet, because Jerusalem is the city of the great king. The battle for Jerusalem is the battle for sovereignty over planet earth.

At the beginning of this chapter I stated that the nations are God's idea. With Yeshua's return all nations are put under his authority and *"the kings of the earth"* are judged. This does not mean that the office of "king" no longer applies within each nation. The Scriptures anticipate the kings of the earth being judged for their rebellion, but also that a day will come when the rulers of nations will willingly submit to God's rule:

"Nations will fear the name of the LORD, and all the kings of the earth will fear your glory." (Ps. 102:15)

"All the kings of the earth shall give you thanks, O Lord, *for they have heard the words of your mouth, and they shall sing of the ways of the* Lord, *for great is the glory of the* Lord.*"* (Ps. 138:4–5)

"Kings of the earth and all peoples, princes and all rulers of the earth…let them praise the name of the Lord, *for his name alone is exalted; his majesty is above earth and heaven."* (Ps. 148:10–13)

The one who created the nations judges all the nations, but just as is the case with Israel, in the end he redeems the nations as well. The rebellion of kings is transformed into worship, praise and songs of adoration. As the Scriptures testify, Yeshua is *"the ruler over the kings of the earth"* (Rev. 1:5 NKJV). Therefore, He appoints new kings to provide national government under the planet wide authority of the King of Kings. Revelation 19 describes the destruction of the kings of the earth who arrayed themselves in battle against Messiah Yeshua. In Revelation 21, the Kings of the earth appear once more; this time, not in rebel alliance but as those chosen to rule, who bring into the holy city of the New Jerusalem *"the glory and the honor of the nations"* (Rev. 21:24-26). In that day, when *"the* Lord *will be king over all the earth"* (Zech. 14:9), the Sovereign Lord will still share his rule over the planet with humanity, the creatures made in God's image to have dominion over the earth.

CHAPTER 14

Joint Heirs with the King

Every blessing in the Hebrew prayer book begins with the same refrain: "Blessed are you LORD our God, King of the universe…" There is no disputing God's sovereign reign over all creation – He is the king of the universe and has always been the ultimate sovereign. With God's choice to create a creature made in His image and likeness He expanded His capacity to rule into a new dimension. The One who is always sovereign over all, could now rule through independent god-like creatures that would function as regents delegated to rule under His authority. The Sovereign's direct rule over the universe could now potentially be expressed through the agency of another. The King of the universe could also rule the universe indirectly, through relationship with a creature made in His image and likeness.

Creation began with *"and God said…and it was so."* There was no intermediary between the word going forth from the mouth of God and the execution of His will. But with the creation of humans who resemble God in capacity and identity, the word spoken by God could be received and complied with by choice, or it could be rejected. The word God spoke, *"of the tree of the knowledge of good and evil you shall not eat"* (Gen. 2:17), did not ensure compliance with the directive. Sadly, this word spoken by the one who spoke all creation into existence was not obeyed. That this was even possible is a tremendous witness to the ability and the authority of human beings. I reckon that to be made in God's image and likeness is far greater in capacity, creative power and even in majesty and glory than anyone has yet to fully comprehend.

Human beings are unique creatures in the universe because they have been created to rule. We understand from Satan's

147

opposition to God's will, that like human beings angels can, or at least could refuse to do God's sovereign bidding. However, angels were never given a mandate to rule. The Hebrew word for angel is also the Hebrew word for messenger.[123] They are powerful beings but always in the role as servants, they were never given the authority to rule on God's behalf.[124]

God created mankind to rule over planet earth, over all the other creatures, over all the resources and over every dimension of territory of the planet. The fact that even in our diminished capacity as sinners, we have been able to reach beyond the confines of our atmosphere, indicates our capacity for dominion could possibly extend beyond our planet to worlds yet unknown.

The extent of God's intentions for us to rule under His authority is boundless. As the Scriptures testify, *"Eye has not seen, nor ear heard, nor have entered into the heart of man the things which God has prepared for those who love Him"* (1 Cor. 2:9 NKJV). The divine pronouncement, *"Be fruitful and multiply and fill the earth and subdue it, and have dominion over the fish of the sea and over the birds of the heavens and over every living thing that moves on the earth"* (Gen. 1:28), should be understood more as a magnificent gesture of love and generosity to be received, than a command to be obeyed.

The premise of this book is that the rule extended to humanity was always to be a delegated authority under the ultimate authority of the Creator. By submitting to God's rule, the rule of God on planet earth would flourish as a shared reality between Creator and creature. This sort of sovereignty would necessarily leave room for human creativity and an obedience that could potentially express itself in multiple varieties, born out of multiple human experiences. How humans subdue the world in a tropical environment would be quite different from humans obeying the same directive in an artic environment.

---

[123] Hebrew: *malach* (מַלְאָךְ). i.e. 1 Sam. 23:27
[124] Ephesians 1:21 speaks of ruling powers. 1 Corinthians 15:24 indicates Yeshua will destroy these ruling powers when He returns to rule on earth. Therefore on can deduce that satanic powers are in view.

The example need not be so dramatic. Human obedience to God's commands is as varied as each human being. Isaiah and Jeremiah both obediently spoke the word of the LORD to Judah and Jerusalem, but their prose reflected their own individual personalities. So too, human beings filling the earth would uniquely express God's rule according to their unique personalities, experiences and identities. Extending sovereignty to human beings did not in any way diminish God's authority over the universe. It expanded it, in the sense that the obedient response of humans would by virtue of the human condition, create a multi-hued response, commensurate with an ever-expanding multi-faceted human story.

The Creator's magnanimous gesture of conferring dominion over the earth to humanity resulted in a tragic choice by those first humans. They continued to be creatures made in the image and likeness of God, but now the oneness that they enjoyed with the Creator and with each other became marred. Each individual human from that time forward became a separate arbitrator of what was good and what was evil. Even if someone attempted to always do good, apart from God imparting His wisdom to know the good, every person would still fall short of doing good. What may appear good for one could in fact be detrimental not only to oneself but especially to others. When the relationship of oneness is broken selfishness, pride and greed are sure to follow. When we do not inherently understand how our actions and words impact on others, our capacity to function for the common good is greatly diminished.

Human beings do not have the capacity to consider all the ramifications of their actions. We cannot know all things; we are trapped within the confines of space and time, and even to some extent in our own individuality. We learn from experience whether our decisions, even the decisions we thought were good were in fact the correct choice. The tree in the midst of the garden was not "the tree of good and evil" but *the tree of the knowledge of good and evil*" (Gen. 2:9). As finite creatures, after we partook of the fruit of this tree we learned this knowledge by experience. In order to protect us from learning what is good by first experiencing every evil, we needed a rule outside of ourselves to guide us into what is right, and steer us away from what is wrong.

But our history has demonstrated that even when we know what is good and what is evil we still often choose what is evil and reject what is good. The consequences of the first disobedience changed our disposition. After our *"eyes were opened"* (Gen. 3:7) by partaking of the fruit of the tree, we still needed our Heavenly Father's guidance to choose the good. But now, instead of a total reliance on Him to reveal the good, our newfound capacity to choose for ourselves blinded us through our newfound self-interest. When oneness is shattered, relationship is broken. Our new reality as independent creatures, disconnected from God and disconnected from each other, hindered our ability to receive and obey the commands of God, the "rule outside of ourselves."

The expressed truth of God, His Torah written as commandments could not remedy this internal problem.

> *"For what the law could not do in that it was weak through the flesh, God did by sending His own Son in the likeness of sinful flesh, on account of sin: He condemned sin in the flesh, that the righteous requirement of the law might be fulfilled in us"* (Rom. 8:3–4 NKJV)

Our inability to obey the Torah because of our weakness *"through the flesh"* required a remedy that only God could supply. However, because the problem was a change in our internal disposition, that is, our *"flesh"* corrupted by our sin, the remedy required a human solution. Therefore, the one who would strip away the Serpent's usurped authority, transform humanity and restore the created order was required to be born of *"the seed of the woman"* (Gen. 3:15).

And so, the one who created humanity in His divine image and likeness, who endowed us with the capacities to have dominion over His creation was also the same one who brought a solution to the human problem. Yeshua, the man from heaven (1 Cor. 15:47), restored the divine order in creation set off kilter by human frailty. Yeshua, the Word made flesh (John 1:14), overcame human weakness by taking on human weakness.

"Being found in human form, he humbled himself by becoming obedient to the point of death, even death on a cross. Therefore God has highly exalted him and bestowed on him the name that is above every name, so that at the name of Jesus every knee should bow, in heaven and on earth and under the earth, and every tongue confess that Jesus Christ is Lord, to the glory of God the Father." (Phil. 2:8–11)

The solution to our disposition towards disobedience was achieved through the Messiah's obedience. What Adam failed to do, Yeshua did, thus reversing the curse on humanity brought on by disobedience. By taking the lowest place Yeshua was raised to the highest place and given all authority in heaven and on earth (Matt. 28:18). Yeshua, the God/man did what no one else could do.

"The righteous requirement of the law" (Rom. 8:4) is obedience to the law. It is the will of God that is done in heaven also done on earth. Yeshua's obedience, even to death on the cross served as a priestly intercession. This not only satisfied the justice required by human transgression, by lifting the curse it set in order the conditions necessary to bring about our required inner transformation. The New Covenant cut in Yeshua's blood writes the Torah on the human heart. It accomplishes the internal solution to the internal problem.

However, the issue of authority on earth is not only an internal problem in the heart of each person. Human beings make socio/political and environmental choices that affect all life on the planet. These choices either conform or rebel against the sovereign will of God. As the one raised to the highest place Yeshua receives sovereign rule over the planet. When Yeshua takes his rightful place as ruler of the planet, the will of heaven will be done on earth as it is done in heaven.

Yeshua is Lord of all. He is not only the saviour who rescued us; He is God's appointed king who because of his obedience receives all the earth as his inheritance. Though this was all according to the will of God, at least hypothetically, we should not assume Yeshua's humiliation and death was necessary for his exaltation. Before the Son submitted to the Father's will to take the lowest place he already enjoyed the highest glory. The glory Yeshua received in his resurrection was *"the glory that* [he] *had with* [the Father] *before the world existed"* (John 17:5).

Further, it was through the Son that the world was made. *"All things were made through him, and without him was not any thing made that was made"* (John 1:3). As the Creator, the Son already had ultimate authority over the planet because *"the earth is the Lord's and everything in it"* (Ps. 24:1). Yeshua had to *"suffer these things* [to] *enter into his glory"* (Luke 24:26) only because it was the will of heaven that not only Yeshua enter into his glory but all of redeemed humanity as well. All that Yeshua suffered was solely for our sakes. He could have ruled over this planet as the Lord of glory without the cross. The planet belonged to him. It was only because his suffering would restore humanity's authority on the planet that it was necessary for him to endure the cross. It was only and all for us. Yeshua would still be king without us, but Yeshua is our Great High Priest so that we can reign with him.

As God's appointed king, Yeshua receives all the nations as his inheritance (Ps. 2:8). He will *"have dominion from sea to sea, and from the River to the ends of the earth"* (Ps. 72:8). He made it all, it always belonged to him, but he receives it as an inheritance as the son of David, the king of Israel, the King of Kings. He receives it as a man so that mankind can join him in his rule.

We who belong to him serve him as our Lord and King and yet, we also reign with him as joint-heirs together in Messiah. We *"have received the Spirit of adoption as sons, by whom we cry, 'Abba! Father!' The Spirit himself bears witness with our spirit that we are children of God, and if children, then heirs—heirs of God and fellow heirs with Christ"* (Rom. 8:15–17).

"For it was fitting that he, for whom and by whom all things exist, in bringing many sons to glory, should make the founder of their salvation perfect through suffering. For he who

sanctifies and those who are sanctified all have one source. That is why he is not ashamed to call them brothers…Since therefore the children share in flesh and blood, he himself likewise partook of the same things, that through death he might destroy the one who has the power of death, that is, the devil, and deliver all those who through fear of death were subject to lifelong slavery." (Heb. 2:10–15)

From the beginning it was God's good pleasure to share his reign with us. We chose to reign for ourselves (or so, we foolishly thought), and as a result became ensnared in bondage. He freed us from that bondage by submitting to the Father to be made perfect through suffering. He suffered so that we could be sanctified together with him. Despite the sad history of the human race he is not ashamed to call us brothers.

When God created humanity in His image and bestowed on humanity the authority to rule, He did so with the anticipation that humanity would rule through receiving revelation of what is good by virtue of our relationship with our Heavenly Father. The decree to endue humanity with the authority to rule on earth was not foremost a matter of obedience, it was an overture of love. To receive the revelation of what is good from our Heavenly Father goes far beyond ensuring obedience and correct action. If the Creator was only concerned that His will be done on earth as it is in heaven, He could have ensured that His will was done by appointing angelic mediators to instruct humanity regarding Heaven's will for planet earth. Instead, God chose to create humans in His image and likeness who would lovingly respond to His goodness and wisdom to ensure His will was done.

By creating beings through whom He could rule, God expanded the circle of relationship heretofore only experienced by the Father, the Son and the Holy Spirit. God made us to rule not so much that we would rule as obedient delegated regents but that we would share in His creativity, oneness and love. The restoration of authority on earth not only assures that God's will is done on earth as it is in heaven, it brings to fruition the promise,

153

"And I will walk among you and will be your God, and you shall be my people" (Lev. 26:12).

Yeshua took the lowest place on our behalf because it was always the goal that not only creation would be restored but also that humanity would be consummated. For us, this will mean the answer to Yeshua's high priestly prayer: *"that they may all be one, just as you, Father, are in me, and I in you, that they also may be in us"* (John 17:21). It was always the Father's good pleasure to give us the kingdom (Luke 12:32), because ultimately, to be one with the Father and the Son is to rule and reign with them.

The restoration of humanity's rule over planet earth is the restoration of the oneness we shared with God in the beginning – but it is much more than that. It is that oneness consummated, we will partake of the tree of life and live forever, one with our God. It is not the end, but a new beginning of wondrous possibilities as we, the joint heirs of Messiah join him in his rule. As the Scriptures declare, *"we shall also bear the image of the man from heaven… what we will be has not yet appeared; but we know that when he appears we shall be like him"* (1 Cor. 15:49; 1 John 3:2).

The wonder of this love that transforms us into the image of *"the man from heaven"* is almost too much for us to consider, certainly it is too vast and glorious for us to fully comprehend. To be one with the Father and the Son as they enjoy oneness together is also to share in the glory the Son enjoyed with the Father before the world began. As Paul reminded the Romans, *"the sufferings of this present time are not worth comparing with the glory that is to be revealed to us"* (Rom. 8:18). Yeshua, the Lord of glory took on flesh and blood, submitted to death on the cross, was raised from the dead to the highest place, received all authority in heaven and earth - and did all of this to raise us up with him as joint heirs of all things.

> *"Oh give thanks to the LORD, for he is good, for his steadfast love endures forever! Let the redeemed of the LORD say so… Let them thank the LORD for his steadfast love, for his wondrous works to the children of man!"* (Ps. 107:1,2,8)

SCRIPTURE INDEX

156

ABOUT THE AUTHOR

Marty Shoub is an itinerant Bible teacher currently serving as a director with Return Ministries, www.return.co.il and as the Canadian representative of Tikkun Ministries International. www.tikkunministries.org.

Marty Shoub graduated with a BA honours in theology from Briercrest College in 1989 and a Masters of Jewish Studies from Messianic Jewish Theological Institute in 2015. Marty is a co-leader of the Loving God Blessing Israel initiative. www.lovinggodblessingisrael.com.

Marty Shoub is also the author of "To The Jew First: The Formation of One New Man" available at Amazon Books. You can contact the author at: MartyShoub@tikkuninternational.org